The Lost Diaries of Constantinople

THE LOST DIARIES OF CONSTANTINOPLE

Author: Mehmet Coral

1st Edition / October 2008 / ISBN 978-975-991-987-0
Certificate no: 11940

Translation: Birol Oğuz
Cover design: Yavuz Korkut
Print: Mega Basım, Baha İş Merkezi A Blok,
Haramidere Avcılar - İSTANBUL / TURKEY

Doğan Egmont Yayıncılık ve Yapımcılık Tic. A.Ş.
19 Mayıs Cad. Golden Plaza No. 1 Kat 10, 34360 Şişli - İSTANBUL / TURKEY
Tel. +90 212 246 52 07 / 542 Fax +90 212 246 44 44
www.dogankitap.com.tr / editor@dogankitap.com.tr / satis@dogankitap.com.tr

The Lost Diaries of Constantinople

Mehmet Coral

DK DOĞAN KİTAP

To Süreyya, Hidayet
Fahamet and Ayla

Not knowing how to seek out and speak the truth is a flaw that can never be concealed by knowing how to speak of the untrue.

Boris Pasternak

Foreword

As we stand on the threshold of the new millennium, one of the most illustrious cities of all history celebrates its own twenty seventh century. I briefly wrote of some of the turning points in the epic history of this city in the foreword to my book *Vanished Epochs in Byzantium* In that work, I wrote of the city's one thousand one hundred and twenty nine years of Byzantine identity which was already drawing to a close when the Turks entered the city on that morning of the 29th May in 1453. In this book I have attempted to bring to life sketches from those audacious centuries of Ottoman rule where, even when the name of the city was modified slightly to *Constantiniye*, it never failed to lose its significance as the 'city of Constantine'.

This book's overriding concern has been how, in the extraordinary life-time of Sultan Mehmed II, this nomadic fiefdom of the steppes became to be an empire straddling three continents. When Sultan Mehmed II conquered the city he was not just seizing the last remaining fourteen square kilometres of what had once been the Eastern Roman Empire, but he was, in effect, putting his own stamp on the Roman concept of empire, something that had been the dominating cogency for close to two thousand years. Apart from the fact that the city had been the first to accept Christianity as a state religion, it had, for the Western World, come to be the symbolic custodian of so many concepts and ideas of crucial importance. The conquest of the city brought to an end the Middle Ages with a resounding jolt that so shook the kingdoms of Europe that they began to fear for their very survival. Thus it was that the year 1453 became seared into the consciousness of the West, so much so that even the mention of it could invite the bad luck that this black year had now come to embody.

The shock waves of the conquest of Constantinople have also travelled down through the ages. At the beginning of the 19th Century and following Napoleon's Egyptian campaign there was an explosion of interest in Egyptology and everything Egyptian. In the decades that followed and even into the twentieth century, scholars such as Davidson, Aldersmith, Habermann and Wynnes would propound theories that within the extraordinary structure of the Great Pyramid itself was to be found an archive of history, past, present and future. From their studies of the Great Pyramid they concluded that one of the greatest disasters to have befallen humanity was the conquest of Constantinople by the Turks. They then interpreted the vertical line starting from the ceiling of the great gallery to represent the defeat of the Ottoman forces at the battle of Luleburgaz on the 27th and 28th 1912 which effectively put an end to the Ottoman presence in Europe. They then brought their sparkling scholarship to its heady conclusion by interpreting the granite slab at the north end of the side chamber as signifying the final capitulation of the Turks with the signing of the Treaty of Sèvres on 10th August 1920![1]

The young conqueror was a mere twenty one years of age when the city fell to him. With a level of intelligence bordering on genius mixed with an equal measure of naked ambition and consummate cruelty, tempered with his love of the arts and sciences and not to mention his passionate love affairs, the young Sultan raised the columns on which the edifice of the new empire would rest. The concepts of state principles that he established continued to be efficacious at every level for close to five hundred years. When one considers the stumbling attempts at democracy of today's political life and the inability to introduce it into all organs of the state, I strongly believe that no time would be lost and everything would be to gain from looking back and studying Sultan Mehmed the Conqueror's methods in organising the nascent state. We must relinquish from the collective consciousness the fossilised shell of official history and the myths, or the creation of myths, behind which is concealed the realities of that age.

I have, in some episodes of this book, tried to emulate the

1. Abandoned in favour of the renegotiated Treaty of Lausanne following the nationalist victories in the Turkish War of Independence and thus forming the foundation of the present Turkish Republic.

Amazonian Indians with their long slender blow-pipes; but in place of poisoned darts I have used my pen to launch a few well aimed ideas towards the readers mind. These might cause a burning sensation when they hit their target and, if really poisoned, they could prove mortal. The reason I have chosen to aim my 'darts' during the course of these episodes is that the events themselves are so momentous in their scope that, if I were to go into every minute detail, they could become swamped in the ebb and flow of history.

At times, it is extremely difficult to fathom the brilliance of the Ottoman state when, in a stroke of genius, the pirate Barbarossa is made admiral of the fleet and leads the Ottoman fleet to one of its greatest naval victories at Preveza in 1538 for then, a few short years later in 1571, only to hand the fleet's command to the Janissary commander Muezzinade Ali Pasha, a man who had before never left dry land, when there was a highly experienced sea wolf like Uluç Ali, champing at the bit to take the command. The result was the disastrous defeat at Lepanto, fought against the combined fleets of the Holy League.

It is to this end that I have presented some episodes of the diaries in a condensed pill form. Sometimes it is the right angle and the right lighting in a photograph that ignites the imagination far more successfully than the subject alone. I have endeavoured to allow the reader the approach that suits them best.

I have presented the events as extracts from a collection of diaries rather than as narrative. As in my previous book, *Vanished Epochs in Byzantium*, I have allowed true events, real people and the correct chronology to tell the story without destroying the sense of time and place. The narrative that Istanbul tells of its past is so full of dramatic incident that it would be beyond any writer to try and conjure up anything as compelling.

As we try to make sense of the fading pages of this city's past, the city itself perpetually continues to shroud the lost diaries of its inhabitants, past and present, in a veil of mystery.

Boğazkesen
(The Cut-throat Fortress)

Georgios Tesaloniko, the Byzantine emissary, persevered with reciting his Emperor's titles from the thick parchment scroll that he held in both hands by, eventually, coming to the point:

"...Lord of Mora and Thrace, Sovereign of the Queen of Cities of Constantinople, Imperial Majesty of the Roman Empire, His Highness Constantine Palaelogos Dragases the Ninth brings to the attention of the exalted Sultan of the Turks, Mehmed Han the Second, the fact that..."

The young eyes of the brooding Sultan burned like fires as if at any moment a bolt of lightening would crack down from where he sat perched on his throne in the midst of the royal pavilion. A fact that did not escape the emissary who hurriedly tried to complete his reading of the scroll with more than a distinct tremor in his voice and a tremble in his hand. The young Sultan turned slowly to Saruca Pasha, who sat at his right hand and who was also a commander of his forces, and addressed him in a loud voice:

"Tell me Pasha, do you think their emperor who, by all accounts, rules the whole world can save these sorry souls from returning to Constantinople with their heads tucked under their arms?"

Large beads of sweat started to roll off emissary Tesaloniko's brow as he hurried to get to the bottom of the scroll.

"...It has come to our attention that there are plans afoot to construct a fortress in the district of *Laimo Kopian* and, lying as it does within the borders of the Holy Roman Empire, for the great Turkish Khan to consider such a rash act can only be construed as being of hostile intent by our side which, in turn, could only have a detrimental effect on the warm relations established between our two great empires by your illustrious father, the late Sultan Murad II. We therefore demand that the construction of this fortress cease forthwith..."

One fury filled glance at his commander was all that was needed. Saruca Pasha, as well as being the Sultan's commander, was also his uncle too. The pasha gave a rapid hand signal to his men who grabbed the Byzantine emissary and his attendants by the scruffs of their necks and the seats of their britches and threw them at the feet of the Sultan. The wrath of the young Sultan rolled around the pavilion like a thunder storm.

"You pompous fool, your hideous smirking faces will be all that I will require as a reply to your exalted emperor! Perhaps then he will refrain from sending emissary after emissary to try and tell me what I can and can't do in my own realm! Pasha! Have their heads cut off right here and now and then have them tied under the arms! Mount them on their horses, but spare the life of their grovelling groom so that he can lead their excellences back from whence they came! Dispatch a squadron of our cavalry to accompany them as far as the *Genoese Podesta* at the entrance to Galata. And one final thing, make sure that you don't fail to show the right level of respect to his imperial majesty's emissaries! Make sure that everything is done in a way that reflects the glory of Master Constantine himself!"

So saying, he swept out of the royal pavilion without a heed to the cries for mercy emanating from the prostrate emissary and his men. Saruca Pasha hastily gave the instructions to his men to carry out the sultan's orders and then quickly followed after his sovereign nephew. The sultan started talking to him even before he caught up.

"Well, what do you think, dear uncle? Will Master Constantine dare to send another emissary? And do you think we will hear any more objections to our fortress?" Without waiting for a reply from his uncle he continued to vent his anger. "Anyhow, it is really of no importance, we will continue as we know best; but make sure you complete the tower designated to you before either Halil[2] or Sogan[3] does, after all we share the same blood and I would hate to see you shamed in front of your own men!"

What he may have lacked in years, Sultan Mehmed made up

2. Çandarlı Halil Paşa (Chandarli Khalil Pasha).

3. Nick name for Zağanos Paşa (Zaghanos Pasha).

for in guile; he had the cunning of a fox and could easily play off, one man against the other, in this case the three pashas who commanded his hundred thousand man army and thus, he had his fortress commanding the Bosphorus built in record time. The towers and fortifications of the fortress to be constructed on the craggy Bosphorus cliff would give the startled observer the appearance of a mural.

Only four short months previously, Sultan Mehmed had called for his old tutor, Aksemseddin, to seek out his opinion of a dream he had just had. Building on the tutor's interpretation of what he had seen, he had formed in his head the plans for a fortress to choke off the vital supply lines for the beleaguered city coming from the Black Sea. The site for the fortress to cut off the Bosphorus from the rest of the world was as clear as the nose on his face. The Byzantines called the place *Laimo Kopian* or 'Cut-throat' and that name was eminently appropriate, there was to be no further discussion the fortress would be called 'Cut-throat'! It was at the same point where, some two thousand years before, the Persian King Darius had made a pontoon bridge across the Bosphorus by lashing together his galleys. He had a throne hewn out of the same rocky cliff so that he could look down on his army as it crossed from the Asian shore to that of the European one. For Sultan Mehmed no such problem existed, his army was already round about him, he just wanted to make sure that there were some sufficiently high fortified towers for the hellfire that the Hungarian foundry master Urban's cannon would rain down on the Latins' ships, thus cauterising the main supply artery to Constantinople.

One morning some weeks before, on the heights above the Byzantine village of Estiai (today's *Arnavutköy*) Sultan Mehmed was discussing strategy for the coming siege with his commanders. They sat in the shade of the tall trees that filled the yard of the Hagia Mikail Church. The sultan had a stretched buffalo hide brought to him and, with an iron glowing white hot from the fire, he rapidly and without hesitation branded the whole plan of the fortress he had envisaged onto the stretched hide.

"There, my lords, is how my fortress will be constructed. The tower closest to the water will be Halil's, the one above and to its left Zagonos's and the one to the right Saruca Pasha's. Work on the foundations will start simultaneously. The first to complete his tower will first receive Allah's blessing and then mine. Each of you will be responsible for requisitioning your own building materials. If you so wish you can even pull down the religious buildings there and use the stone blocks for your project without paying heed to anyone's tears of supplication. If any of you are wondering why have chosen the fortress to take this form then I suggest when it is completed you view it from across the strait, from the fortress my great-grandfather Yildirim Bayezid constructed. You will then observe that it traces the letters 'Mim-Ha-Mim-Dal', the same letters that make up the name of our blessed Prophet and also, coincidently, of mine, his humble servant. Signifying that this fortress will remain the lock on the Bosphorus door until the end of time. Furthermore, every gate will be embellished with the letter 'Mim', the letter that begins the first seven verses of the Holy Quran, the initial letter of our revered Mohammed as well as of your Sultan Mohammed, thus may our holy venture be duly blessed. And now my lords, to work!"

Cambazhane Kapısı
(The Circus Gate)

The cicadas whirred incessantly in the stifling glaring heat of the afternoon. As was their usual practice, the men of the neighbourhood gathered in the coffee house close to the walls of the *Burmalı* Mosque. They had seated in their midst a young man with a vivid scar down his face. As the young man spoke they listened intently, nodding their heads from time to time. Not so much as a leaf stirred in the trees. There was no respite from the searing July heat of Edirne. One of the elders rose and gesturing towards the garden addressed his companions.

"My friends, let us retire to the shade of that great willow out there, perhaps there will be a breeze to bring us a little relief. And call to the keeper to refresh our jugs of *Ayran*[4] and may the lion's share go to young Ali here, in equal portion to the courageous deeds he did in that, the most auspicious of sieges!"

After they had settled in the shade of the ancient tree, the same elder turned to the young narrator again:

"Now, *Demirci* Ali pray continue with relating this mighty epic, tell us how this venture all began and how it was concluded with that supposedly impregnable bastion of the non-believers, falling eventually to our fearless warriors!"

Before commencing Ali took a long draught from the jug of *Ayran* that had been placed before him.

"The smoke from the gunpowder, so dense it appeared almost like a solid mass, hung over the city like a blanket. The siege had been continuing for exactly fifty two days. It had been close to two months since our army first set out from Edirne with such great ceremony on the 23rd of March, reaching the outskirts of

4. Yoghurt drink.

Constantinople, at a place called Hebdomon, on the 4th of April. The sultan, in his wisdom, decided that only one day of rest would suffice and so it was that the siege proper started on the morning of the 6th of April.

I was signed up to the company of irregular Bashibazouks. We never did learn the exact number, but our officers would boast to us that our army was over a hundred thousand strong . Men coming from all of different manner of backgrounds and with varied experience. In the Bashibazouks, this meant they could be anything from porters to shepherds and *muezzins*; from farmers to bath attendants and ruffians; from hell-raisers to dervishes and teachers, as well as Christian renegade adventurers in a quest for fame and fortune. In short, there were men of every walk of life and nationality. We had been gathered up from the towns, villages, fields and valleys; some enlisted straight from their work places or from farms, and even straight off the street while on their way back home. For a number of weeks the town-criers, or *Tellal*, had been announcing that joining the Jihad, which our young sultan had called against the infidel, was to be a chance of a lifetime for all the faithful and, if we were truly the fortunate servants of Allah, we might even taste the sweet nectar of martyrdom. But then again, if we were not so fortunate as to go straight to Paradise, then we would at least receive both the reward of being a Ghazi, or survivor of a holy war, and the indescribable plunder that this, the city of cities, offered us.

Before we set out on the march, the officers randomly handed out weapons. The luckier of us received swords, pikes or maces, the others were told to fend for themselves. Some brought scythes and sickles others, like me, the tools of their trade, hammers and the like. Those who could not find even these primitive weapons were employed in supplementing the oxen by helping to pull the huge canons, cast by the renegade Urban the Hungarian, on our long march from Edirne to Constantinople.

As I said the siege started after one day's rest and from the very earliest days, our officers constantly goaded us on by getting the Bashibazouks to throw themselves against the walls of the city, whose high towers pierced the skies, crying out 'Allah Allah Allah' as we did. The city's defences consisted of three levels of walls with a fosse and moat between. We, the Bashibazouks, were thrown into what seemed like an endless number of assaults. Many took that sweet draught of eternal life in the murky waters of the moat until their bloated bodies eventually formed a causeway over which their comrades could cross.

Day and night we threw ourselves at the walls without respite, we fell like leaves in an autumn gale and were squandered by the thousand. With the light of each dawn Urban's guns would thunder out, crashing down cannon balls on the infidel's seemingly impenetrable walls. Then we would say 'could this day be the sacred day our master the Prophet has spoken of?' And so saying we would cry out until our lungs would burst and throw ourselves at the walls anew. We stumbled, we were cut down, we perished in the process but we could never breach those walls. On one of those dawn barrages Urban was blown to pieces by one of his own cannons along with twelve other brave men. Their limbs were thrown high in the air and came down to earth like a shower of rain.

Following our evening meal the imams would harangue us with the same sermon each night, they would tell us that the good tidings of the Prophet were nigh and how blessed were the soldiers of our army and what bliss awaited the warriors who tasted the sweet nectar of martyrdom!

'God help us!' we would mumble each night as we curled up to try and sleep under the dome of the stars; these we would attempt to count as the madman attempts to count the hairs on a sheep skin. Tossing and turning we would slip in and out of dreams of death. Fear and belief emulsified in our minds so that the only escape seemed to be our own demise. The smell of blood and rotting corpses hung in the air slowly deranging the sanest of us. We would talk to ourselves constantly. Sometimes one of the men would wander out into the fields of no-man's-land and when the sergeant would haul them back by the scruff of their necks and demand what they thought they were doing, they would reply that they were just going out to check the crops and would be right back! Or others might say they were just going to collect the stars they had shot down with their slingshots! There comes a point where reason melts like ice in the sun. There was none of us that could not wait for an end to this mortal coil so that we could taste the clear waters of Paradise that had been promised us. Death would obliterate the nightmares and relieve our souls of our tortured bodies.

Every night too, a new fantastic rumour would spread amongst us like wildfire. Each mouth would swear it to be true; had you heard? A mystic named 'Cebe Ali' had thrown the sheep skin he used as prayer rug on to the waters at Galata and standing on it glided across the waters to the Byzantine sea wall. As he approached he raised his mighty scimitar above his head causing the terrified soldiers manning the walls to fall back dumbfounded, but just as he was about to bring his sword crashing down on the walls he paused and said 'this is not the time!' and turning, glided back across the water. And on a number of other occasions word spread that when the time came all the blessed fallen of the Prophet's army that had been buried at the foot of the walls all those years before would rise from their graves and following the Prophet's standard bearer, the blessed Eyyub el-ensari, mount the walls and open the gates for our army! You know what they say about mystics? One never knows what they'll do next!

We began to feel that the siege was drawing to its conclusion. It became the stuff of legend when gathered round the mess tent in the evening to talk of how our Sultan had said "either I take the city or it takes me!". We all knew that we would only remain alive if we could breach those walls in front of us. We were living cheek to jowl with death. The giant cannon that we called '*Şahi*' and the enemy called '*Vasiliki*' had all but destroyed the 'Haghios Romanos' gate in the Likos valley. It was for that reason we had given it the name '*Topkapı*' or Cannon Gate. We were told that it would require only one more frontal attack to surmount what remained of the wall and enter, what had been pledged to us, the promised land!

With the first light of dawn the drums of the *Mehter* band began to beat out their stirring music. Our sergeants mixed words of encouragement with blows from their canes to push us forward for the ultimate assault. As with the previous fifty two days it was the Bashibazouks who were to be the expendable cannon fodder, although now down to almost their last man, to fill the fosse with their dead and exhaust the enemy thus allowing the final assault on the infidel's insurmountable walls.

Stumbling over bodies covered with swarms of bluebottle flies we managed to get our ladders up against the enemy walls and crying out 'Allah Allah Allah' we began our slow climb upwards as the infidel began to pour down boiling oil from above, instantly scalding many of our men. Others were more horribly disposed of by being hit by molten lead that seared the flesh away from the bone. Screaming like demons, some tried to haul themselves back across the swollen corpses to get back to our lines but the sergeants were waiting there to finish them off and throw their corpses into the fosse so adding to the ones that already had been used to fill it. For some reason I, and about thirty other fellows, were spared these horrors by pressing our backs against the wall but, nevertheless, coming within a hair's breadth of a most horrible death by what was being thrown down from above. We then started edging our way in the direction of the Golden Horn.

At that moment, the second wave of the assault commenced, led by the Anatolian brigades and the dismounted cavalry. They roared like lions as they started their attack. They were well trained soldiers and started to beat back the enemy. At this point we saw the most celebrated soldier in the whole army, *Ulubatlı* Hasan, all two metres of him, with a handful of soldiers make it to the top of the wall. We came back and tried to mount the same ladders only to see Hasan's enormous body hurtling down from the wall still clutching the standard in his hand. He crashed into the ground head first, his helmet flattened by the impact. We were then caught in a volley of arrows and many of our number were struck down. The remainder of us once again flattened ourselves against the wall. Once again, with our backs against the wall, we edged our way toward the Golden Horn. Now armed with the weapons we had collected from Hasan and his fallen comrades we began to give ourselves more than a few heroic airs.

Still edging forward at the foot of the inner wall it was not long before we found ourselves beneath the walls of the infidel king's palace. All was quiet there but, by a stroke of luck, I noticed that there was a small door set into an angle where a tower projected from the wall, but more importantly the door stood slightly ajar. We carefully made our way to this small armoured door and when we applied our shoulders to it, the door slowly opened inwards. On the other side of the door was a winding stair which presumably went up to the tower. Nothing could stop us now and we took the steps two at a time and tumbled out onto the deserted summit of the tower. We looked down below on the heavy hand to hand fighting which was taking place further along the wall at the Miriandrion gate *(Edirnekapı)* and when our soldiers fighting there looked up and saw us, they almost swallowed their tongues in astonishment.

After this moment of surprise, our comrades returned to their life or death struggle with renewed vigour. One of our small band had taken with him the standard that Hasan had refused to let go of as he fell from the walls, this comrade now climbed up to the highest point of the tower and, jamming the pole into the turret, unfurled the flag. In a blink of an eye twenty arrows found their mark on the poor lad's body, but it was now too late as our flag still fluttered in the wind. The waves of enemy soldiers that were in the process of making a counter attack looked up and stopped in their tracks. An eerie silence followed. This was followed by a shout from the midst of the most fiercely contested point, it was a shout filled with the pathos of utter despair:

'*Alosis Poleos!*' (The City has fallen!)

From that point on it was Armageddon for the defenders of the city. Wave after wave of Janissaries breached the walls as the defeated enemy fled in chaotic confusion towards the centre of the city. I looked down on the rout leaning my weary and wounded body against a turret and thought to myself: 'Strike me down! Will you just look at the ways of almighty Allah! Could you have imagined that amongst all those decorated heroes of a thousand campaigns, who should plant the flag on the insurmountable walls of Constantinople but a bunch of country lads!'"

The young man, *Demirci* Ali, sat back and took a deep breath. He lifted the jug to his lips and finished the *ayran* in one gulp. He dabbed his lips with the back of his sleeve, patted his knees and rose to his feet.

"The rest you all know. How the city was sacked and so on. I fear you have made me talk too much. Now if you'll excuse me, and may peace be with you all." So saying he touched his breast with his right hand, bowed and left.

Epistola ad Mahumetem II
(A Letter to Mehmed II)

With windows open to the breezes from the Golden Horn on one side and the Bosphorus on the other, the suffocating July heat did not feel quite so oppressive in the audience chamber of the Imperial Palace. In addition, the sultan's throne was fanned by four Nubian slaves holding large peacock feather fans. It would have been difficult to describe the throne as ordinary, gilded as it was and decorated with precious stones as, in the same way, ordinary would not have been the word that described the young monarch who sat upon it. There was a hint of sarcasm in the smile that brushed his lips as he read the letter held lightly in his right hand. Without raising his head he addressed the elderly man who stood before the throne with his head bowed and his hands clasped tightly before him.

"Do you hear this master Patriarch, if I so desire he could award me the title of king of the East and the Eastern Roman empire. Would you credit it, what an extremely impressive man I have become!"

Before the elderly man wilting in his heavy vestments had an opportunity to comment, the door was flung open and a chamberlain approached the throne and, genuflecting nine times in accordance with an ancient Turkish custom, announced the arrival of the Grand Vizier, the Grand Mufti and other religious dignitaries. The Sultan responded to this news with an almost imperceptible nod of his head.

When the gathering entered the chamber they were seated, heads respectfully bowed waiting to be addressed, on the side of the chamber facing the Golden Horn. The Sultan toyed with his thin beard and looked at each one of them in turn with a piercing stare. He turned to his chamberlain and told him to summon the Lady Irene from the Harem. Still with their heads bowed there was no discernible reaction from gathered company, only the Grand Mufti mumbled 'God Almighty!' just loud enough for his master to hear. Sultan Mehmed did not comment but thought to himself: 'Today your account could be settled here too, you boot licking cleric!'

On the day that the city fell, when Sultan Mehmed entered in triumph on his white steed to make his way to Hagia Sophia, he caught sight of an equestrian statue of the Emperor in the middle of the large square called Agusteion. The statue stood on top of a high plinth with the Byzantine Emperor portrayed holding a globe surmounted with a cross in his left hand and with his right hand he stretched out to the West.

After the life and death struggle of the fifty two day siege this was what occupied the sultan's mind now as he sat on his horse in front of the statue. He imagined their roles reversed, but instead of a cross on the globe there would be a crescent moon, and instead of a frozen bronze mount, he would be on his white stallion prancing forth to become conqueror of the world in the direction which the late Emperor had so charitably indicated. This was the burning ambition that had kept him enthralled since he was a child and, just as he was loosing himself in this reverie, he recalled the dry words of his old tutor, Aksemseddin.

The old man had instructed him that the statue was of the Emperor Justinian who had given the order for the construction of Hagia Sophia in the 6th Century. His tutor had read to him from the historian Procopios, a contemporary of Justinian, from his work *Edifices*. There the historian described how a column of some forty thee metres height had been constructed on a seven step plinth made of huge blocks of marble; the column was then covered, as was the custom of Roman emperors, in spiral bronze plaques depicting, in relief, the victories and achievements of the Emperor. The Emperor himself was depicted as the Greek god of war, *Ares*. During the Fourth Crusade when the Latins occupied and looted the city they removed the bronze plaques and melted them down to make coinage to pay their soldiers. There was still a similar monument to this at the south end of the hippodrome.

The young conqueror shook his head to rid himself of his tutor's dusty words and turning the head of his steed galloped over to the mighty doors of the Great Church itself. He dismounted from his horse, bent down and picked up a handful of dirt and raising his hand above his head trickled it onto the top of his white turban and then to the cheers of his soldiers he entered that breathtaking edifice.

As he recalled these events the door to the audience chamber opened once more and, wearing a simple blue silk dress, an extraordinarily beautiful and dignified woman entered the chamber. Her silky fair locks hung down as far as her waist and her thin veil only made to emphasise more, the brightness of her large green eyes. She passed in front of the clerics with the correct propriety and took her place close to the throne. The two young lovers exchange a brief exchange of glances. For an instance the sultan's eyes flared up and then died with the fire of a crazed hopeless love. Then, speaking formally, the sultan bade the young woman to sit at his feet. She gracefully and silently complied to his command. The sultan then turned to the others who had been following this all closely. They sat kneeled with their hands deferentially clasped in front of them. The sultan began to address them with more than a small measure of sarcasm in his voice.

"My lords, I have received a letter from Rome, from the emperor of the unbeliever's Catholic Church, his holiness Pope Pius II, in which he has made me a lavish offer, the Patriarch Gennadius has translated the letter and will now read it to you."

The sultan thrust the parchment at the elderly man waiting at the foot of the throne. The Patriarch bowed to the Sultan and then turned to face the assembled clerics.

"My lords, as his majesty the sultan has instructed..." He turned to bow to the sultan again who waved at him to continue. "...I will leave out the long introductory section and read to you from the most pertinent part:

> ...You should be fully aware that I harbour no hatred towards you. In our faith we are bound to love our enemies as ourselves and that includes the slayer of that selfsame faith; I constantly pray that you will learn the error of your ways and find the true path. You should also be aware that you cannot bring under your yoke the Latin kingdoms as easily as you did those of the East, such as the Greeks, the Serbs, the Wallachians and other non-believers. However, if Sultan Mehmed really wished to expand his sovereignty into the kingdoms of the West and to raise his stature still further then there would be

no need of money, weapons, armies or fleets. Just one small gesture could make you the greatest and most powerful mortal upon the earth. And if you ask what this might be? The answer is not difficult at all. There is no need to search far and low for it. It is found everywhere. Just a little water or 'Aquae pauxillum' will make you a Christian to make you a servant of God and the Gospel and having done that not one prince on earth will surpass you in glory and power. We shall name you Emperor of the Greeks and the Orient, and what you have for now obtained by violent means and hold unjustly, will become yours by divine right. All Christians will honour you and make you their arbiter in their disputes. The oppressed will look to you as their protector and ask for your succour; people will come from all over the earth to submit to your sovereignty, paying homage and tribute to you. You will be called upon to crush the tyrant, protect the poor and drive out the deceitful. You will be seen as the world's protector. And if you walk along the true path the Church of Rome will never oppose you. The occupant of the highest position in Christianity will bless you and you will be the first amongst all the monarchs. And thus, without war or bloodshed you may acquire many new kingdoms. We would never give succour to or help your enemies; on the contrary, we may call on you to punish those who use the faith for their own ends or who revolt against the mother Church. If you were only to convert...[5]

With a sharp gesture the sultan interrupted the Patriarch's words and spoke instead.

"Etcetera, etcetera. The rest is all in the same vein. My lords, you have heard his Holiness the Pope's lofty offer. So what are we to do now? To bring the Latin kingdoms to their knees must we leave the true path of Allah and prostrate ourselves before the cross? It is as though the Orient and the Greek Empire was not ours already, as if we needed the Master Pope's approval for this?" He paused and now looked directly at the Grand Mufti. "It has come to our attention that there have been rumours emanating from the offices of the Grand Mufti, his eminence the Sheihk-ul-Islam, and from other clerics that I have forsaken my faith,

5. The text of the original letter was taken from the Vatican archives. It was translated from Latin into Italian on the 500th anniversary of the conquest and published as Pio II: Lettera a Maometto II (Epistola ad Mahumetem II), by Guiseppe Toffanin, Naples 1953. There is no historical evidence as to if the letter Pope Pious II wrote to the Conqueror ever reached its recipient or not. We find the tragic story of Irene in the work of writers such as Young, Babinger and Saint-George.

that I engage in drinking bouts and orgies and that I am besotted with a woman who refuses to convert to our faith. Let it be known to all and sundry that we have the strength to utterly destroy anyone who has the audacity to slander our religion.

The young sultan slowly rose to his feet and with such fury surging up in him it was as if bolts of lightening would start fly from his eyes. Those in the chamber began to cower imagining this to be the beginning of one of the sultan's infamous rages. Their bowed faces instantly drained of blood imaging that at any moment they would feel the greased cord of the *Bostancıbaşı*[6] encircling their necks. The Sultan hauled the beautiful Irene to her feet from where she had been sitting at the foot of the throne. She had come to his notice immediately following the conquest of the city when the overseer of the hastily erected slave market in the Arcadius Forum carefully selected her as tribute for their conqueror. The sultan had, in an instant, fallen madly in love with, what surely must have been, the most beautiful maiden in the whole of the city. But, ever since, however much he tried he could not get her to denounce her religion and embrace his.

"Raise your malicious viperous heads and look at me!" He roared at the assembled.

The clerics had, by now, laid themselves prostrate at his feet with fear. They slowly lifted their heads to look as their sultan commanded. The sultan gently lifted the veil from the young woman's face.

"Have you ever, in your wildest dreams, ever thought you would come so close to such perfect beauty? I love this woman more than life itself! However, that life has already been betrothed to Islam and so, it seems inescapable to me that I must sacrifice this life for my faith!"

So saying, and to the complete horror of the terrified clerics, he pulled out a dagger that he had concealed at his waist, and jerking the young woman's head back by her hair, he cut her throat with one florid stroke.

6. Bostancıbaşı: Lord high executioner

The Freeman Architect Sinan[7]

The traffic hardly moved in the stifling summer heat on the broad avenue that leads from *Unkapanı* to *Saraçhane.* Even with all the windows open, the middle-aged man at the wheel used a handkerchief to wipe his copiously sweating brow as he tried to encourage his companion.

"Hardly anything left now, we are nearly there. As soon as we pass under the *Bozdoğan Kemeri* (Valentinian Aqueduct) we will take the first right towards *Fatih.* After that, depending on the traffic, it shouldn't take us more than ten minutes to get to the *Kumrulu* Masjid. You realise that after all this effort, it is hardly a work of great architectural importance that will greet us? *Kumrulu* Masjid is a comparatively recent building, very ordinary with little to its merit. It got its name from the adjacent fountain. There is a marble relief with two doves, they're depicted drinking from the fountain of eternal life. It is supposed to be of Byzantine origin. However, a few hundred metres further on is the *Nişancımehmetpaşa* Mosque. Now there is a little known classic of Ottoman architecture, a veritable jewel box of a building! Let's go straight on to there after we have seen the *Kumrulu* Masjid."

The traffic had began to flow and the middle-aged man at the wheel turned the vehicle westwards after passing under the arches of the viaduct and up into *Fevzipaşa* street. The traffic slowed to a halt before once again flowing so that they soon passed the south wall of the *Fatih* Mosque complex and turned right into *Yavuzselim* street; from there they went straight ahead for about a hundred and fifty metres before turning right again where they

7. Called 'Atik' or Freeman to distinguish him from the later and more celebrated 'Koca' or great Sinan.

pulled over to the side of the road and parked. The two friends got out of the car and walked over to the iron railings that surrounded the masjid.

"So this is it, the tomb of the freeman architect. He is laid to rest under those two carved gravestones there."

"I see it now, a plain but extremely moving monument, in my opinion. And how very strange, it is as though he still wanted to reach out and communicate with the people who visited it. The calligraphy on the gravestones is quite stunning too, could you translate it into modern Turkish for me?

"Now let's see here, reading from the right to the left of course. '*With God's forgiveness...*'". He turned to his friend and smiled with his finger still pointing at the characters. "I am fooling you, I can't read Arabic script any more than you can, but I have learnt what it says by heart."

"Tell me then, from your heart please!"

"All right, it goes something like this:

> With God's forgiveness and with his endless grace, the freeman Architect Sinan, passed from this mortal world into the everlasting life on the twenty seventh day of the eight hundred and seventy six Hijre year (13th September 1471) by being martyred at the dark dungeon at the shore's edge, in the night following evening prayers some time between Thursday and Friday. May God protect him from the afflictions of the grave and damnation.

The two friends remained silent for a while, both looked through the iron railings at the two grave stones. It was as though for five hundred years the drama of this man's passing was rekindled for every new visitor alike.

"You have studied the architect's story, perhaps you could fill in a few of the details for me?"

"I could try, but the freeman Sinan is almost anonymous. There are almost no historical records to draw on and those that do exist, mere fragments. The Ottoman accounts are the stuff of legend with some fantastic decoration thrown in. The Greek ones are mere exaggerated scraps of information. If one tries to splice together the threads of both accounts then you end up with this, by way of a biography:

Nobody has ever been able to find out the name he was born with. The Greeks say that it was 'Christodulos', Ottoman sources say 'Abdullah'. The interesting thing is that they both have the same meaning, both in Greek and Arabic, namely 'servant of God'. Very enigmatic wouldn't you say, the veil of anonymity for the 'servant of God' who built so many of the fine buildings dedicated to the Almighty. One thing is certain though, six hundred years ago this individual was born somewhere within the borders of the Ottoman Empire. We know nothing of his family or his Christian origins, all we know was that he was indentured in the spring of his childhood. He entered the adult world in the city of the same, Constantinople. He was instructed in the Islamic religion and was given the name Sinan, a popular name for converts at that time as it also meant 'spear', so that the holder was also, by association, the 'Spear of Islam'!

It seems he felt the creative urge from an early age. He took an intense interest in the world around him, he always wanted to build things from anew, to reform and reshape them. He started from the bottom, working as an apprentice labourer, breaking stones, mixing mortar and building walls; from there to a mason and from there to becoming the master architect himself. The richness of his design filled the buildings with space. After a number of years he was made a freeman. The Conqueror of the world's greatest city and the ruler of seven kingdoms, Sultan Mehmed Khan recognised his consummate skill and made him his chief architect. He was given the task of repairing the badly damaged dome of Hagia Sophia and restoring it to its former glory by converting it from a defunct church into being an even more glorious house of God (a mosque) so that the crescent would now be seen to supersede the cross both on its dome and in its splendour.

The freeman Architect always looked first for the grace of God in his labours and then for that of his patron. For days and nights he studied and surveyed this sublime structure that, with its immense size and extraordinary dimensions that had stood for over a thousand years. When he had completed his surveying he set to work. In order to realise this monumental mission of converting this house of God, from its function as a church into that of a mosque, he had to commit every waking moment he possessed to this extraordinary project.

The freeman Architect applied the same level of dedication to the construction of what later became known as the *Fatih* Mosque. He built it in, for that period, the remarkably short time of only seven years and eleven months. Little remains of his masterpiece now apart from the surrounding building complex as the main structure was badly damaged and later demolished in the great earthquake of 1766 and the current structure was built at the orders of Sultan Mustafa II; and all the experts agree that what we see today bears little resemblance to the original.

They say that the original masterpiece was as full of light as a summer morning and as pure as a child's prayer and as inspiring as the contemplation of immortality! It was with his customary humility that he welcomed his master the sultan when he came for the building's inauguration. He presented his finished masterpiece to him and in doing so, at the same time, dedicated it to Islam.

The sultan nodded and then started to survey the building in a state of rapture, an edifice that would bear his name for posterity. But after a short time his rapture began to turn to wrath.

'I ordered you to make my mosque higher than Hagia Sophia, but you've actually had the temerity to make it lower by cutting the height of the columns, each of which, I might add, cost as much as the annual tax of all the conquered lands, you've clearly done this on purpose!' The sultan bellowed in the architect's face.

The freeman Architect was completely taken aback by this, while he had been wishing for no more than a few words of gratitude he had, instead, been assaulted with this wild accusation. Furthermore, the sultan had been a constant visitor to the site during its construction, he had taken a close interest in every aspect and they had even spent many an hour discussing the construction in detail together. The sultan had always expressed his greatest desire was that, more than anything, his mosque should stand for all eternity.

'My sultan,' the architect attempted to explain, 'Because of the constant threat of earthquakes in our city and to protect the structure from any possible damage, I decided to lower the columns by just three cubits making the dome imperceptibly lower than that of Hagia Sophia.' On hearing this the sultan's fury knew no bounds:

'You have just compounded your calumny with this stupid attempt at an excuse!' He gave the order for the Architect's hands to be hacked off right there and then. As The freeman Architect watched his hands, the means by which he expressed his creativity, made his living and praised God, severed from his wrists by the executioner's sword, his world ended. He was a broken man.

He lived for another three years just the shell of the genius he had once been. One September evening in 1471 he was arrested and dragged from his home for no apparent reason. He was thrown into a dank, smelly former Byzantine dungeon at the shore's edge. There he was beaten to death. As he lay dying, he appeared to suffer no pain from his broken and twisted body for he had long lost all physical feeling, as from the moment his heart was shattered under the lofty dome of his last masterpiece."

The Demon Prince Vlad

The royal council had been in session since morning. The council members, well versed in the sultan's notorious rage, sat cowered, as the though from the gathering storm clouds of wrath that filled the chamber, might come the bolt of lightening that could signal their demise. The news from Wallachia had made Sultan Mehmed furious. An upstart of a prince was causing havoc in the region. Not only amongst his own people but reports had come in of outrages against Turks too. Two weeks earlier, in an attempt at a diplomatic solution, envoys were sent but nothing further had been heard of them. The sultan turned his attention towards the council chamber doors which were now opened slightly ajar. Mahmud Pasha discretely hurried to the door where one of the *Hasağa*, or heralds, imparted some whispered communiqué. Mahmud Pasha turned and bowing towards the throne announced that the envoys had returned from Wallachia and requested an audience.

"Let them in immediately!" The sultan cried clapping his hands.

Three dishevelled looking men were ushered in. Their clothes were in tatters and they bore the signs of fresh wounds on their heads and arms. The most senior of them knelt before the sultan and then kissing the hem of his robe waited prostrate before his sovereign. The sultan poked him with his foot to prompt him to rise. The sultan then sat back and inspected the three sorry envoys before addressing them angrily.

"My lords, did we send you on a diplomatic mission or did we send you to make war? We sent thirty of you and only three of you have returned? And where is your head envoy, Hasan Pasha?

I think you have a lot of explaining to do!"

The senior envoy clasping his hands before him in supplication, rose from his knees, took a deep breath and began to explain what had happened.

"My liege, in accordance with your command we journeyed to the land of Wallachia to convey your demands to Prince Vlad also know as 'Vlad the Impaler'. The Wallachians came out to meet us at a place called Braila. They offered us hospitality in a large castle in the foothills of the mountains. They kept us there for a week without ever bringing us before the prince. Hasan Pasha became extremely agitated and demanded, as the personal envoy of the Ottoman Sultan Mehmed II, that if he was not offered an audience immediately he would pack his bags and leave. He made it clear that such a situation would only go to ignite his sultan's wrath still further. The prince's servant told us not to concern ourselves as the prince would be able to receive our delegation almost immediately.

During the week while we were kept waiting Hasan Pasha would go out and wander around the town's market to sound out what was happening. He chanced upon a Saxon knight who related things about the prince that were, at first, almost impossible to believe. He said that it was his habit to drink human blood and that his greatest pleasure was to see people being slowly impaled and as they writhed in their agony he would dine and drink wine with his entourage. He also told of how one day the prince invited all the beggars from across the country to a feast in his castle. He laid out a sumptuous banquet in a church hall and then joined the beggars in their feasting, drinking and merry-making. Towards the end of the feast he excused himself, had his men lock and bolt the doors before having the building set alight so that those unfortunates inside were burnt alive.

On another occasion when the prince was strolling around a market he came across a group of women nursing their babies. At first he patted a few of the babies on their heads before turning to his men to comment that the babies were not being fed correctly and that they would never grow up to be warriors, he therefore ordered his men to nail the babies to their mother's breasts. A monk who witnessed this horror and expressed his outrage was immediately impaled to his donkey for his impudence.

The Saxon knight did not stop there he related that Vlad, on receiving the answer 'I'm not sure', from one of his concubines when the prince asked if she was carrying a male heir, the prince proceeded to rip open the poor woman's womb with his bare hands saying it was the simplest way to find out.

On another occasion when inspecting a group of newly impaled victims one hot summer's day, an aristocratic member of his entourage asked the prince how he could stomach the stench; the prince gave orders for the unfortunate and over-familiar lord to be impaled on the tallest stake they could find, adding that from that height he wouldn't smell a thing."

Mahmud Pasha bent forward and whispered into the envoy's ear that he should cut the embellishments short and get to the point of what happened to them. The sultan, realising what he was saying, interrupted him.

"Let him continue, I'm intrigued to know to what lengths of cruelty the infidel can possibly go. Continue, my lord"

"As you wish your Highness. On another occasion, 400 youths were sent to this heathen's country from Hungary and Transylvania, the purpose of their visit was for them to learn the local language and receive instruction. One day the Impaler appeared before the foreign students and said that not only was he going to be their instructor for that day but that he was also going to teach the most important lesson of their lives. He collected them into a large hall and then told them all they needed to know could be summed up in one sentence and that was that they should be totally merciless towards their enemies and destroy them at the earliest opportunity. He then turned and strolled out of the hall giving orders at the doors for them to be locked after him and the building set alight!

And that is not all, there was a mass impaling of six hundred traders from the Burcia region just because they had the audacity to bargain when they were buying and selling cattle. Then there was a banquet he threw for five hundred *Boyars*, or feudal lords, and then because none of them knew the exact population of their fiefdoms, he had the lot of them impaled.

But, my exalted sultan, there is no end to the excessive cruelty of this monster, so let me finish these bloody anecdotes right here and tell you exactly what befell us.

On the eighth day Prince Vlad's henchman came. He told us that his prince was ready to receive our delegation and then led us to the palace. We found the prince in the courtyard observing and apparently savouring the screams of a new victim going through the grisly process of being impaled. He sat with his back to us. We were kept waiting like that, for some considerable time. Finally Hasan Pasha edged forward a few paces so as to attract his attention. Immediately the guards jumped forward to bar his way. At that moment the Prince turned his demonic head to see what was happening, said something to his men and turned his back again. One of the prince's henchmen came across and told the Pasha that first he should remove his turban and bow down in obeisance. This was the last straw for the Pasha who loudly protested that he made obeisance to no one except his sultan and that his turban never left his head. Hearing this, the devil personified rose from his seat and slowly approached the Pasha, a smirk of pure malevolence infecting his face. And then with sneering deference he prodded the Pasha's turban and said:

'My noble lord, I do wonder if that turban of yours really is firmly on your head?'

At first the Pasha did not understand what he was trying to imply and then, when the horror of it dawned on him, he responded valiantly. 'By God, it is!'

Without removing the same ingratiatingly evil smirk from his face, the prince turned to his men. 'Well, I, for one, am not sure. You check it for him and, if it is firmly on his head, bring him to me. If it is not firmly in its place, straighten it for him and then, making sure it is well secured, bring him to me.' So saying he turned his back and returned to watch the grotesque torture.

Before we knew what was happening the soldiers had grabbed hold of Hasan Pasha and pinned him down, another group of soldiers surrounded us and held us at bay with razor sharp pikes. All we could do now was watch with dread what was going to befall him.

The soldiers dragged Hasan Pasha to where the prince sat. He gave the pasha a disdainful look and turned to his lackeys: 'I am still not convinced that the pasha's turban is securely on his head, what do you think?'

They laughed jeeringly and to a man they brayed: 'How right you are majesty, the Turk's turban doesn't look secure one little bit!'

The monster beckoned to two of his henchmen, they stepped forward in front of him..."

At this point reliving these dreadful events proved too much for the elderly and wounded envoy and he started gasping for breath. The sultan gestured for water to be brought and a bowl of water was placed to his lips. He started to talk again but this time with some difficulty.

"The two men stepped forward, one held a large hammer while the other carried three thick blunt nails. Hasan Pasha, realising what was to befall him, began to struggle. He shouted out in desperation:

'What do you think you are doing you monsters! Know this though, my master, the ruler of the whole world, will never allow his envoy's blood to be spilled unanswered!'

Everything happened in an instant, and while their accomplices held the unfortunate pasha, they drove three nails, one after the over, through the turban into the poor man's skull. Still with a look of horror and disbelief in his eyes life quickly drained from the pasha. They picked him up and threw him at the prince's feet. The prince of darkness downed the remainder of the wine in his goblet and then lifted the pasha's head with the toe of his boot. With the same demonic look on his face he addressed the lifeless head of the pasha.

'There now! That's better isn't it? Now nobody can remove the turban from your head, lord of my boots!' And he started to laugh uncontrollably while his lackeys all joined in the satanic mirth.

They threw us in to a disgusting dark dungeon that we shared with rats as big as cats. Each morning a leering guard would come and randomly chose three of our company and have them taken out. As he slammed the iron bars shut he would call out:

'Today the pleasure falls to these three, have no fear each one of your arses will have their turn!' Four days later we seized our chance and managed to escape our captors, on the way back we lost three more and all those that remain are before you now."

The days of horror, fear and deprivation had taken its toll. Willpower must have kept him going just long enough for him to deliver his report and, that duty having now been discharged, the old man's heart gave out and he collapsed sideways in a heap on the floor.

Sultan Mehmed sat frozen with his forefinger resting on his lip he stared into the distance. The fire had gone from his eyes and in its place there was now an icy glow. After some considerable time he rose to his feet and first pointing to the envoy at his feet, he addressed his council.

"Raise this unfortunate servant and, with all the dignity that the state can muster, give him a funeral that will do him justice. As for the other two, tend to their needs, give each one a purse of gold and let them spend a couple of months with their loved ones; after that get them to report back to their barracks." He turned to his Vizier:

"Mahmud, mobilise the army immediately. The campaign season has come early. I mistakenly allowed this monster a free rein as long as he paid his tribute. I even helped him with his domestic politics, I aided him in overcoming a rival to his throne. We have never acted rashly, we even hold his brother here in Constantinople as a bond, but now the dogs of war have been unleashed. Now is the time for retribution for this knave. I swear on the blood of my martyrs that if I don't have this bastard impaled on a stake in front of my pavilion while I eat my dinner, let me be damned!"

"Your command will be carried out to the letter, my liege!" The Grand Vizier Mahmud Pasha said, jumping to his feet. The other members of the council rose to their feet in accord, only the sultan's private secretary, Yunus Bey, a man of Greek origin who was also known as Tomas Katavelunus, remained seated. When he felt the sultan's eyes come to rest on him he also rose to his feet. The sultan, continued to look at him straight in the eyes and Yunus was forced to lower his head. Always strongly intuitive, the sultan addressed Yunus:

"If you had something on your mind you would say it, wouldn't you, Yunus?"

Yunus was left no choice but to speak of what he had been thinking.

"The decree is yours my sultan, what more could your humble suggest only that perhaps, cunning can be mightier than brute force on some occasions."

The sultan, with one sweep of his hand had the council chamber cleared. He turned expectantly to his private secretary. Yunus Bey knew his master well. The sultan had no time for empty words and he always expected rapid and intelligent answers to his questions.

"My liege, let us invite this infidel to the Seraglio." Yunus said. "We can tempt him with an offer of sovereignty over the whole of Wallachia in addition to Hungary and Transylvania. However, for this he will have to come to Constantinople. We can demand as a gesture of goodwill that he bring with him 500 youths as a gift. We can appear to wield a stick by demanding that he pay the ten thousand gold Ducats of tribute that are currently in arrears. Your majesty will in return for this make him vassal of all Wallachia and Moldavia. Military support can also be offered if required. Your personal secretary along with a squadron of troopers could meet him at the border to accompany him to Constantinople where he would be greeted like a great monarch and showered with gifts. All of these, just bait and empty promises, of course; we would trap him as soon as he crossed the Bulgarian border. Thus we would be saved the expense of a great campaign not to mention the lives of many of our brave young soldiers."

Sultan Mehmed was taken by Yunus's plan. He looked out from the window stroking his thin beard before turning to his Vizier.

"Yunus has spoken a lot of sense. Dispatch a messenger straight away to *Çakırcıbaşı* Hamza Pasha, governor of the Danube region, get him to raise a brigade of his finest assault cavalry and to wait for Yunus's arrival. Don't give any details of this operation to anyone and if I hear of anyone getting wind of what we have spoken of here, in my dreams even, I will have you both hoisted up on stakes higher even than Constantine's column, so at least you'll get a fine final view of the city, bear that in mind!"

Only two weeks after Yunus's departure for Vidin news of the disaster that followed reached the palace. The trap that Yunus had devised had failed drastically. Voivode Vlad the Impaler came pre-warned and acted with ruthless precision completely destroying Hamza Pasha's cavalry. Some of them managed to escape but Yunus and Hamza were captured. Vlad first had their hands and feet cut off and then impaled them. In recognition of their rank, Vlad made sure that they were placed on higher stakes than the other victims!

Vlad having come so close to falling in to this trap went insane with anger. He raised an army and set out to lay waste as much of Ottoman territory as he could. He crossed the Danube and put to the sword and burnt any settlement he came across. Women, children, the defenceless he made no distinction, all were horribly slaughtered. It was said that he captured over two hundred and fifty thousand soles, all of which after terrible torture were impaled. Breaking the news of these terrible events fell, as always, to the unfortunate vizier Mahmud Pasha. The sultan, who at times of crisis displayed remarkable cool-headedness, on this occasion snapped and vented his anger out on Mahmud Pasha. Before he could finish speaking the sultan rose from his throne and started thrashing him with his cane after turning his wrath on the closest members of the council. It was only when the cane broke on one unfortunate's back that he regained his self-control. He sat down heavily, put his head into his hands and started to think. He raised his head, wiped the sweat from his brow with the sleeve of his caftan and addressed the council with his customary authority.

"Mahmud Pasha, send out word to all four corners of the land. We are to raise an army equal in size to the one we employed in the siege of this city. I want them to be armed and made ready for campaign. Supplies and reserves will be taken by the fleet up the Danube and will set sail at the same time as the army starts on its march. May I be damned if I don't send this Satan, impaled on a stake, back to the hell that he came from!"

On the 26th April 1462, Sultan Mehmed watched his hundred thousand strong army setting out for the campaign from the tower at the Edirne gate. He himself was going to set sail later that day in the fleet's flagship. He had taken command of all aspects of the campaign. After Vlad had been deposed of, he would add the lands of Wallachia to his empire, just like he had done with Serbia and Greece. He was taking Voivode Vlad's brother, Prince Radu, with him. His plan was to put him on the throne as a vassal in place of his brother as soon as he had secured victory.

Radu had become a favourite of the sultan's during his stay in Constantinople. The boy's fair pink complexion and his good looks had never failed to attract the sultan. On one occasion, after having lain with the boy, he asked him how his brother Vlad the Impaler, could be so remorselessly cruel. Without raising himself from where he lay on the bed the boy answered in a languid voice.

"You should understand better than anyone, how many times do you impale me when we lie together?"

The sultan considered this for a moment and wondered if Vlad inflicted his cruelty in such a way because he had been sodomised at some time in his earlier life. Come what may, he thought, this was certainly the way he was going to end it, and on the tallest stake that anyone had ever seen.

After the army had passed Edirne but was yet still some way

from Philopopolis, Sultan Mehmed had arrived with his fleet and entered the Danube where they raised the city of Bralia, Wallachia's largest port. He disembarked his troops and started to advance into the hinterland. They were met by the strangest landscape. The towns and villages they came across in the Wallachian plains were all deserted, there was no sign of any resistance. The only people they ever saw were the very elderly or simpleton shepherds. Sultan Mehmed began to feel uneasy. One evening in his tent he raised his concern with his vizier.

"If this continues it will look as if we raised an army for nothing. Where is this demon Voivode? Where are his people? My intuition tells me that we should be very careful. What do you say Mahmud?"

Mahmud demurred, pointing out that the next day they would meet up with the main army and then, even if Vlad grew wings, there was no way he was going to escape his fate.

Indeed, the next day they did meet up with the main army and now the combined Ottoman army was a force of over one hundred thousand men and they moved across the plains like the blade of a scythe. But this new optimism lasted a mere day because the plains soon ended and they were confronted by dense oak forests and impassable mountains. Sultan Mehmed realised what Vlad had done. He summoned his commanders and summed up the situation for them.

"This demonic Vlad the Impaler is more clever than we imagined. Before our armies arrived, he withdrew all the population, livestock, army and supplies and hid them behind these wall-like forests and mountains. He is holding his forces back behind the mountains waiting for us to advance into the forest where every tree will become like an enemy soldier for us. His familiarity with the lay of the land of his own country he will use this to his advantage and inflict great losses on our army. We, however will continue and advance on our prearranged course because when we have taken the rest of the country he will be forced to show his hand. And, when he does, he won't know what has hit him."

The sultan's estimation of the situation was correct. Vlad had less than ten thousand soldiers to call upon. The only way he could take on the might of the Ottoman army was with hit and run tactics, ambushes and surprise attacks. He used the restrictions of narrow Transylvanian mountain passes to inflict losses on the sultan's army. He raided the camps at night while they were performing evening prayers or eating their rations. For the conqueror of Byzantium these were totally new fighting methods, but the sultan was sure of one thing, this was a tactic that could not be sustained for long and that the end of this campaign could not be far off.

On one occasion in the middle of the night pandemonium broke out in the camp. Vlad had chosen to try and take the sultan's tent with a force of three thousand of his finest cavalry. They struck like lightening straight to the heart of the camp where the commanders tents were and killed all who came in their path. The sultan had felt quite secure in the midst of his army and so no trenches had been dug or fires built. Vlad had taken advantage of this and struck the camp like a fire ball. They quickly dispensed with the few platoons of Janissaries deployed as guards and reached the sultan's tent, or so they thought. But the tent was empty . The sultan, despite his apparent overconfidence with security, still took the precaution of having his tent erected at a different position each night but leaving the previous night's one still standing. Without this simple precaution history could have taken a completely different course. Vlad's murderous plans were in tatters. He stood outside the empty tent and screamed so his voice could even be heard over the noise of battle.

"You can't get away from me Mohammed! I will catch and have you impaled on a stake higher that your minarets! I will send your body to Rome as gift for his Holiness the Pope, the worthless corpse of the faith's arch enemy! And he will have you and your inseparable stake hauled up on Trajan's column as a lesson for all and sundry! If you were a man you would come out and fight!"

Outside Sultan Mehmed's tent the Imperial Guard had formed up in a wall of flesh. The army had also regrouped and were now on the offensive. Almost as quickly as the attack had started Vlad and his men found themselves scattering like chickens when weasels are let in the henhouse. The commander of the cavalry, Ali Bey, quickly had his men ready and mounted and was in hot pursuit of the Wallachians. They put a great part of them to the sword but brought back close to a thousand as prisoners. The next day the sultan had them buried alive in a great pit he had them dig in front of his empty tent. They also erected a tall stake on which they placed Vlad's bronze helmet which he had dropped while he was making his escape.

There was now nothing to hinder the army from taking the capital of Wallachia, Targoviste. On the road to the capital there was no resistance at all. When they arrived at the city there was nobody to be seen on the high walls and the gates were wide open. The city had been abandoned. Sultan Mehmed ordered the army not to waste any time with the city but to keep advancing. The earth shuddered from the noise the army made. They had not advanced far when Mahmud Pasha approached the sultan and said that the vanguard had sent back messengers who had reported the most terrifying sight.

"Get to the point, Mahmud! What on earth could be terrifying for these courageous warriors!"

"These men reported that they had just seen the most terrifying and grotesque forest a little way ahead. And yes, they are the bravest of the brave, and yet they were quaking in their boots when they told me this!"

"You are trying my patience, Mahmud! What did they mean?"

"My liege, what they described to me was this: On either side of the road, as far as the eye can see, there is a dreadful forest of impaled Turkish soldiers and civilians."

Sultan Mehmed said nothing but just remained staring at his vizier. He then dug in his spurs and galloped in the direction of the vanguard with his guards and Janissaries close behind. When he got to the place they had described the sultan could not believe his eyes. It was just as they had said. Either side of the road was full of impaled and rotting corpses. He thought he would throw up, but quickly pulled himself together, but his face remained ghostly pale. Without saying anything he gave the signal for his men to follow and he led his mighty army through that avenue of death. The horses got nervous and the soldiers recited prayers without raising their eyes. It took over half an hour to reach the end of that never changing and shocking landscape. At the end of this avenue of death they saw two corpses impaled on stakes twice the height of the others. When the approached they saw that one of them was the Danube region governor, Hamza Pasha, while on the other was the sultan's private secretary, Yunus Bey. They saw another stake behind the others that was even taller still, but there was no corpse on it. The sultan rode closer his suspicion roused. There was a notice nailed to the stake that fluttered in the wind. Mahmud Pasha leapt forward and ripped the notice down with his lance. He bent down and grabbed the paper and as he gave it a quick glance he froze with the blood draining from his face. Sultan Mehmed bent down and snatched the paper from his hand. He then read it aloud in a low voice:

"This stake belongs to the commander of the glorious army arrayed behind, Sultan Mehmed. Very soon he will take his rightful place on top of it."

A strange light came into the sultan's eyes followed by a frightening smile. As he crumpled the paper and threw it away he turned to Mahmud Pasha.

"We shall see about that, if that two legged demon is patient he will soon learn who is going to be impaled on that stake!"

The man who centuries later would become fictionally known as Count Dracula, Voivode Vlad the Impaler, kept up his hapless struggle against the might of the Ottoman Army. But by now his forces had been seriously diminished. Omer Bey in one encounter killed two thousand of Vlad's men and had their heads cut off and thrown at the foot of the sultan. The Wallachian army was all but finished but Vlad still had not been captured. Sultan Mehmed announced to his vizier that the campaign was at an end and it was time to return to Constantinople. Prince Radu was to be made the vassal ruler of the country and he would raise an annual tribute of twelve thousand gold Ducats. A bounty of fifty thousand gold Ducats was put on the head of Vlad, dead or alive, and this was proclaimed throughout the country.

One day, three years later, Mahmud Pasha brought a youth who was studying at the royal inner court school and presented him to the sultan. The youth knelt before the sultan, his hands clasped together in obeisance and waited to be addressed. Mahmud Pasha introduced the boy.

"My liege, this boy was conscripted last year in Wallachia and brought here. He is the son of a Transylvanian priest. I think what he has to retell will be of great interest to my sultan."

The sultan stared at the boy and then snapped the fingers of his left hand indicating the boy to proceed with his account. As it was the first time that the boy had been anywhere near the sultan let alone address him, it was natural that he started speaking with a tremble in his voice.

"My liege, it is as my pasha has said. I am the son of village priest from a mountain hamlet in Transylvania. We were poor, the fields were rocky and barren. We made our living from livestock herding. Our land was ruled by a count whose face no one has ever seen. He lived in the mountains whose summits are zigzagged with lightening, in a castle built on rocky precipice. His men would sometimes come down to take milk and eggs from the village. On every visit they would choose a few young maidens from the village to take with them , they would tell their pleading parents that they were for the 'pleasure' of their lord. The girls were never seen or heard of again. We later learnt that this lord was in fact a demon who sated himself on their blood.

All the villagers in the mountains lived in constant fear. Because they knew that demons were immortal. My father joined the priests from the other villages in long discussions about what they could do to protect themselves. They turned to the bishop of Transylvania for advice and then made their decision. There was only one way to send this demon back to the inferno from which he had come and so they had to lay a trap for him. My sultan, if I am not trying your patience allow me to describe how we rid ourselves of this monster."

The sultan, listening intently, waved his hand for the boy to continue.

"I won't go into detail how we baited and trapped the demon, but suffice to say that it was after many attempts and with a great deal of difficulty that we eventually managed to trap him. We dragged him to the crypt under the church and chained him up. We waited for the Bishop to arrive and when he did he was taken straight to the crypt where he chanted from an ancient book in a language no one could understand. When he had finished he closed the book and stepped back, we threw ourselves onto the count and pinned him to the floor and then a wooden stake was driven into his heart. When at last he stopped struggling and was still, we buried him outside the village throwing quick lime onto the body before we filled the unmarked grave again."

The boy stopped speaking and with his head bowed held out his hand to the sultan revealing something he had concealed in his palm.

"My sultan, this is the medallion that hung round the demon's neck. Before we buried him my father tore it off his neck. When the officers came to take me to Constantinople my father gave it to me and said that when the time came I was to give it to the sultan. That is the reason I am presenting it to you now."

Sultan Mehmed look out of the corner of his eye to where

Mahmud Pasha was standing motionless. He leant forward and took the medallion from the boy's hand. He sat back clasping it tightly in his hand. He then slowly opened his hand and a large grin began to spread across his face. He tossed it in his hand and gave it to Mahmud Pasha.

"And tell me, what is written on it, Mahmud?"

Mahmud, of course, knew full well what was written on it, but nevertheless, he read it aloud in growing wonder as if it was the first time.

"Vlad III, The Prince of Hell!"

Sultan Mehmed jumped to his feet laughing aloud. As he walked towards the chamber doors, he called to Mahmud Pasha.

"Have this young man trained to be my private secretary and have fifty thousand gold Ducats sent to his father!"

Occhiali of Calabria

The flagship, with its satin mainsail emblazoned with three large crescents worked in silver thread, sliced through the morning mist like the point of a javelin. The splendour of the vessel filled the entrance to the Golden Horn. Two men in rich robes wearing honey coloured turbans stood on the raised stern of the ship directly behind the helmsman. As the morning sun suddenly broke through the mist they both raised their hands to shield their eyes scouring the far shore. Neither were in the spring of their youth but, despite their considerable years, each stood erect with a straight back. The lines on the face of the one who now raised a telescope to his eye revealed a life lived to the full. He wore a rich green robe decorated with gold embroidery. He prodded the helmsman with his stick and gave the command in voice that had the ring of authority, of someone used to being obeyed.

"Turn the ship to port. We will pass the Galata jetty and anchor in front of *Karai Köy* (Karai village) the place where the sultan, in his wisdom, has settled the Jewish refugees from Spain."

The helmsman stood bolt upright as though he was nailed to the deck and repeated the command in a deep voice.

"Aye Aye *kaptun*[8] Pasha, steering to port, setting course for *Karai Köy*."

The helmsman, with consummate skill, brought the vessel to its mooring at a short pier close to the shore. The two men walked down the gang plank and then slowly along the strand. Admiral of the Fleet *Kılıç*[9] Ali Pasha paced around flapping his robes and then he halted. Turned his face to the south, that is in

8. Kaptun: Captain.

9. Kılıç: Sword.

the direction of the sea, and struck the ground near his feet with his silver topped cane.

"I want you to construct my mosque right here! On this very spot, Chief Architect *Koca*[10] Sinan. Right across from our sultan's Seraglio and facing that thousand year place of worship, with a dome like the dome of heaven, Hagia Sophia. I want you to build its twin, of course, not on the same scale. I'm no emperor and certainly never a sultan. But nevertheless, I would like my last resting place to have the same *proporzione*, how do you say it? Yes, proportions, of course! The same proportions as Hagia Sophia. The seas could never contain me let's hope this will. There, that's what I want from you Chief Architect."

The great architect had listened patiently while the admiral had spoken with his eyes fixed, all the while, on the extraordinary edifice that dominated the skyline on the other side of the water like some Noah's Ark perched on top of its mountain. He turned to the Admiral before speaking.

"You have spoken wisely Pasha. This place you have chosen for your mosque is perfect. But there is only one thing, please don't ask me to copy that monumental edifice that I have spent my whole life trying to surpass! In my long life I have served three different sultans. Each one of them has said to me, make my mosque greater than Hagia Sophia! But each time I constructed the building they hoped would hold them in eternal favour with God, I always remained true to myself. I never attempted imitation. Please don't ask it of me but allow me to build you a mosque that will do your glory justice instead."

Kılıç Ali bent down and picked up a small flat stone and skilfully skimmed it across the water. He made no attempt at reply. He put his hands behind his back and paced up and down before coming back to where Sinan waited. He sat down cross-legged on the ground and he pointed at a spot beside him for the architect to join him. Sinan the architect sat down cross-legged next to him. The old sea wolf look into the eyes of the architect for whom he had held so much respect for so many years. He then turned his gaze to the sea and started to talk.

"I would be lying if I said that I hadn't lived a long and difficult life. I was born in Calabria in the South of Italy. My parents were unknown to me and I was brought up by a priest. I was told later that I was the illegitimate son of a woman who had thrown her-

10. Koca: Great

self on the mercy of the church, my father was said to have been a fisherman, married to another woman no doubt.

When I was twelve our town suffered a raid from the notorious Barbary pirates. The first person to see their ships was Franco the baker. '*Arrivano i Turchi!*' He screamed, the sound of which, even after close to seventy years, still rings in my ears. Father Giuseppe, my guardian, told me to climb up into the bell tower and start ringing the bell until I was told to stop. I was still wearing my night shirt as I pulled the bell rope as if my life depended on it. Within two hours the pirates had pillaged and burnt most of the town. When they broke into the church my guardian did everything he could to stop them, but for his efforts he was murdered in front of his altar. I was beside myself with fear. One of the pirates tried to grab me, I side-stepped him, but then he caught me around the waist. I can still smell the smell of his grinning mouth full of rotting teeth. I tried to free myself from the vice-like grip he held me in. I managed to get one hand free and grabbed a bronze cross from the altar against which he had pushed me. I brought the cross down on his head. It did little to stop him and when the blood started pouring down his forehead it just increased his frenzy. He pushed me towards the bell tower where the ropes were now hanging still. He wrapped one rope round my neck while one of the other thugs hauled me up in the air. This was the first time in my life I was to see death's white tunnel and, I'm sorry to say, in this long life of mine it wasn't to be the last time!

When I came too, I found I had been chained up below deck in the dark and smelly prow of a pirate ship, they had taken me along with the girls of the town to be sold into slavery. For two days we were tossed around in a stormy sea, housed in a space no larger than a rat's nest, coming close to the point where we would be asphyxiated by our own vomit and excrement. We eventually landed on the Barbary coast and were dragged ashore and, by the way people turned away and held their noses, I realised that we must have smelt and looked worse than wild animals. This was just the first act in this drama of a life that I have lived. For the next ten years I was a galley slave. There was more than one occasion when the skin of my back was flayed from the whippings I received. There were times when the shackles on my wrists and ankles wore through the flesh to the bone underneath.

Have you ever heard the death knell that sound makes? The

sound of rusty shackles striking bone as we pulled the oars? It was far worse than the pain itself.

I danced with death many times during that ten years. And it was towards the end of that period that one day we were caught in a storm. The oarsman next to me keeled over and died from exhaustion and the bastard of a Nubian slave master, who kept us coordinated by beating a drum along with generous lashes of the whip, went crazy when our oar started falling behind. Not realising that the man was dead he rained down blows on his back and then bent forward to bellow in his ear, his foul smelling saliva spraying all over me. I had little reserves of strength and I knew it would have to be finished in one strike. The next time he stopped thrashing and bent forward to bellow in the dead man's ear I wrapped my chain round his neck and pulled. The oaf's neck was thicker than my thigh and I really needed to get another coil of chain round his neck to make sure. It was a life or death struggle as he fought to get his head free but when he lunged forward and I managed to get the second coil over his head then I knew I had him trapped, but he refused to give up the struggle and my strength was waning fast so when he pushed his head forward on to my chest in an effort to free his hands I could see before my eyes the constricted arteries bulging from of his bull neck. At that moment I had only one weapon left if I was to win this battle, my teeth. I sunk them into his neck. He did the worst possible thing and jerked his head back violently so that the chains bit in still further and the hole I had made in his neck exploded like a burst dam, squirting blood into my face, my mouth, my eyes and all over my body. I was all but exhausted when the oarsman next to me said 'Quick get the keys from his belt!', but at that point the thirty stone giant collapsed on top of me; and I, with the foul taste of his blood in my mouth and with the total exhaustion of the struggle, collapsed too.

When I came to my senses I found myself lying on a mat in the fresh air of the top deck. The storm had abated and the sun was streaming through the parting clouds. The other galley slaves told me how they had managed to get the keys from the black giant's belt and, after freeing themselves, had taken the pirates completely by surprise. The ship was now ours, we had gone from galley slaves to pirates and in recognition of my bravery my comrades elected me skipper! *Mare Nostrum* was now really ours.

I took to my new role very quickly, I began raiding and plundering the African coast, choosing in particular the Latin ships with their priceless cargoes that had come via the Levant from India and China and were bound for France, Italy and Spain. The Maghrebi called me *'Olch Occhiali'* . Later, when I was sailing under the Ottoman colours I was honoured with the name *'Uluç Ali'*. And by this name I began to become well known from one end of the Mediterranean to the other. Within a short time I was commanding a fleet of twenty war ships. Because of my close association with legendary 'Red' Captain Barbarossa Hayreddin on the Algerian coast, I became under the patronage of the great ruler of the East. But it was while at the mast with Turgut *Reis*[11] sometimes know as Dragut or the 'Knight of the Waves' that I received the most important lessons of my career.

In 1560 we seized Gerba. Five years later we attacked Malta to where the Knights of Saint John had escaped from Rhodes. But even Dragut's steely determination was not enough for us to take this razor sharp, high cliffed saffron coloured island. Added to which the great Captain himself was martyred in a most unfortunate manner. We took his saintly last remains wrapped in a white shroud and gently lowered them into the sea from which he came and was now returning. His last words had been: *'Sarı Saltuk*[12] carry my soul to God'. So, ahoy there great saint! Have you carried the soul of my captain wrapped in those Mediterranean winds to the place he came from yet?

After Barbarossa's last son passed away and went to meet his maker, the Sultan appointed me the governor general of Algiers. I developed a great hatred for the Spanish and their repression of the Muslim population of the Iberian peninsula. After having destroyed many of their ships on the open seas I then, in 1569 (977 Hijre calendar) captured their most important base in Africa, Tunis. It was such a blow to their pride that they were never able to come to terms with it.

Two years later a messenger arrived from the Sublime Porte, the sultan had called for a holy war against the Crusader fleet. He demanded a repetition of the crushing defeat that Barbarossa had inflicted on the infidel at Preveza, thirty three years before, and that the Mediterranean (the White Sea in Turkish) should become, once and for all, a 'Turkish lake'. We were to witness first hand that witch's cauldron of intrigue that the Seraglio had

11. Reis: Master of a ship.

12. Sarı Saltuk was a legendary Turkish warrior saint.

become, something that would prove the downfall and destruction of our fleet and take the lives of many a brave sailor. In Constantiniye naked ambition made them blind to what was really happening as they stabbed each other in the back in the name of self-advancement!

I had my men scouring the seas for any signs that the Crusaders were gathering their fleet. Eventually reports came back that, for the first time for many years, there were indications of mobilization. Pope Pius V had been successful in brokering a holy alliance. I immediately sent news of this to the sultan. The answer I received back was that Sultan Selim, 'The Inebriated', had considered it of little importance. According to hearsay, he took off his turban in front of the Council of State and said that just as three heads would not fit in the turban, the infidel were incapable of making a pact together.

And to add insult to injury the Grand Vizier Sokollu relieved such experienced sea dogs such as Piyale and Sinan from their posts and made the victorious Janissary army commander from the battle of Mohacs, Muezzinzade Ali, Admiral of the Fleet! If that was not enough, he gave the ageing and chronically seasick, Pertev Pasha, the overall command of the fleet! When I heard this news I felt like crying out aloud: 'You idiots! Do you really think that a skirmish in a river meadow is the same as a sea battle?" Naturally enough, I said nothing and kept my own council.

We learnt that the Holy League's fleet was to be commanded by Don Juan, the bastard son of Charles V and the step-brother of the Spanish King Philip. In my estimation, the infidel had a hundred and ninety galleys and six galleasses. Our combined fleet stationed now near Naupaktos numbered two hundred vessels. However many of them had not sailed for more than six years while many of the others hadn't had their hulls scraped for some considerable time. Many of the crews numbers were made up with soldiers, Janissaries and cavalry troopers who, when given shore leave, had never bothered to return. I joined up with the main fleet in September with my small privateer squadron of three galliots, these I had captured in the seas between Malta and Sicily, along with eight fustas and nine galleys.

Muezzin Ali Pasha called the first war council. I proposed that we avoided battle with the infidel until the spring which would give us time to carry out the necessary maintenance and make sure each ship had a full compliment. I explained that this was the rational thing to do and in no way compromised our honour. Muezzin Ali Pasha caused me considerable insult when he answered by shouting back at me. 'Tell me, is it you Italian blood and the religion you were born into that makes you talk like this? Are you trying to prevent our fleet from utterly destroying the enemy? I shall never let it be said by our sultan that I ran away from the heathens! So what if some of the ships are under manned? Damn the enemy, I say!'

On Sunday, the seventh October 1571 (the seventeenth day of the sixth month 979 Hijre) the lookout in the crow's nest cried out that the enemy fleet was approaching in an extensive line formation. We upped anchor and positioned ourselves into a crescent formation. Agostino Barbarigo held the infidel's left division with a force of 64 galleys. Facing him was the governor of Alexandria, Mehmed Pasha, with a force of 56 galleys. In the centre was Don Juan with a force of 63 galleys and 6 galleasses advancing towards Muezzin Ali Pasha. The infidel's right division was held by Giovanni Doria, nephew of Andréa Doria whom Barbarossa had so convincingly vanquished at Preveza, I held the division that faced him with 63 galleys under my command equal in numbers to the enemy.

Despite my attempts to persuade Muezzin Ali Pasha to take the fight to the enemy in the open sea so as not to allow them to have the benefit of a following wind, the old man only responded by saying that whoever rested their back against dry land would always have the upper hand! The order was given 'full ahead towards the enemy' and as the oars churned up the water the battle cry of 'Ya Allah! Yemliha!' split the air and we headed forth to our own disaster. The enemy had overwhelming firepower. The galliases were like floating fortresses. In a last desperate attempt I dispatched Kara Hoca to Muezzin Ali Pasha. I wrote that the enemy's galleys and galliots are much heavier and less manoeuvrable than ours. If we were to break formation and circled them we could then attack them from the sides and rear. When Kara Hoca returned he handed me Muezzin Ali Pasha's note. He had written: 'I will never let it be said that the sultan's navy fled the battle'.

On each of the infidel's flag ships there were forty four cannon and 2000 fighting men. From the first engagement our ships were beginning to receive serious damage. Most of our ships were armed with nothing larger than arquebuses and could hardly knock more than splinters off the huge hulls of the enemy ships. Muezzin Ali Pasha's only plan was to get close enough to board the enemy ships and send the Janissaries to fight hand to hand. Despite our heavy losses he came close to almost achieving that. The right division of Mehmed of Alexandria had collapsed. I was head to head with Doria. But it was in the centre that the real losses were being felt. Through the smoke I caught a glimpse of Muezzin's ship accompanied by two galleys heading straight for Don Juan's flagship, the Sphinx, which looked to all the world like a floating city. It was impetuous, it was irresponsible, but say what you like about Muezzin Ali Pasha, he had the heart of a lion!

In the inferno that followed they scattered the enemy like so many partridges. Charge after charge, their attacks were audacious, but at that very moment that victory seemed assured, the enemy's reserves sailed around the headland called *Kanlı Burun* or Blood Head. Nobody, including myself, had taken that possibility into account. They started to attack Muezzin and the two other ships. Muezzin now was down to only a handful of men as he launched another attack. Everything reminded one of Hell, the smoke, the fire, the screams and the sound of shattering bones and wood. I disengaged from Doria and took a course south so that I could come round behind the engagement. He thought I was fleeing and, still keeping his distance, started to make chase. After we had gone some distance I gave the order for my ships turn about, taking Doria by complete surprise and slipping back past his ships on either side and so we headed straight to the centre of the action to bring aid to Muezzin Ali Pasha. But it looked as though we had arrived too late.

There were some Venetian galleys who had been watching our approach, they now hauled up their sails and started heading straight for us. My galleots formed a crescent formation. I immediately recognised Giovanni de Macado's red and blue ship the Marquesa, we had had some brushes with each other in the open sea. I was determined to try and board it. But then revised the plan when I realised I would have the other galleys attacking me from behind. But both our ships had come close enough to scrape passed each other at considerable speed. At that moment I caught sight of a one armed officer standing on the foredeck of the Marquesa. He called out to me, addressing me in the Maghrebi dialect: '*Uluch* Captain, today the wind is on my side of the mill! Sheath your sword and get away while you can!' I recalled who he was in an instant. He was a Spaniard from La Mancha whom I had taken prisoner when I captured his galley many years before. He was held hostage in Algiers for five years until he was able to raise the money for his ransom by selling the family estate. He was a man of some intellect. I would visit and talk to him from time to time when he was a captive. He had left his country, family and friends to take part in a holy war against the indomitable Turk only to discover that you might as well pick a fight with a windmill as fight a 'holy' war. He told me that when he had gained his freedom he would return to his native land and write a book, he even had a title for it, Don Quixote. He said that in the book he would put into his protagonist's mouth everything that he had ever learned.

The Venetians left the chase but I saw that we had the Maltese squadron on our port bow lying about a mile to the west. Without a second's thought I gave the order to take a course in that direction. I intended to take out the battle's pain and frustration on those unfortunates. Within a short time we had boarded Giustiniani's *Capitana*. My men went about their business like sharks who have caught the scent of blood. Despite being in my sixties at the time, I held my dagger between my teeth, stuck the flintlock given to me by Barbarossa in my belt and grabbed a grappling hook rope and swung myself across on to the deck of the Maltese flagship along with my men. The fight was over very quickly. We turned our attention to the Venetian galley that had come to the aid of the Maltese and soon had that beaten too. My men were superb, carrying out my commands almost before I gave them. In a short time we had sunk Chippico's La Donna, Jacobo di Mezzo's La Palma and Cornaro's Esperanza and sent them to the bottom of the sea. More ships were coming to the enemy's aid and I began to see we were becoming surrounded and pressed on all sides. I decided to do the unexpected. I made benefit of the Sirocco wind filling my sails and gave the command for my small fleet to set a course to the north. As night fell, taking advantage of the darkness I turned about and took a southerly course slipping past the pursuing Venetians like a ghost in the night.

There were about forty ships left under my command and we reached Constantiniye in fifteen days. I was summoned to the palace. When I was taken before the sultan I presented him with the flag from the Maltese flagship. I swear there were tears in his eye when he accepted it. He announced that I would no longer be known as privateer *Uluch* Ali, but as a commander of the imperial navy and henceforth known as *Kılıç* Ali Pasha. He then said:

'You will seek revenge ten times over from the infidel for every drop of martyr's blood that has been shed. The full resources of the Ottoman state are at your disposal. You and Sokollu will rebuild the fleet together." He then grabbed me and pulled me to his chest. 'My brave fellows, let me see you excel yourselves!' He said.

The rest I am sure you are familiar with *Koca* Sinan. In six months we had launched two hundred and fifty new ships. I had slipways constructed on the Golden Horn as far as the imperial gardens at *Hasbahçe.* But it still proved insufficient so I took over the main squares on all the coastal settlements. I can still hear the sound of, master shipwright, Mustafa Agha's adze ringing in my ears!

There was an exciting sense of competition as the public joined in the race to see which neighbourhood would complete their vessel first. The harbour at Sofianos had been known by that name since Byzantine times, they even changed that because of the glorious galleys that had been built there, calling it *Kadırga Mahallesi* or Galley District.

The following year the fleet set sail. The Spanish had taken advantage of the victory at Lepanto and had retaken Tunis. I obligingly relieved them of it again. I controlled the seas with an iron hand and wouldn't let a bird fly without my permission! I made the sea a very restricted place for the infidel!"

Kılıç Ali Pasha smiled at the memory of this and then let out a deep sigh before continuing:

"But, now I feel my time has come. Dragut, Hizir, Kara Hoca, Salih, Seyid Ali and countless others are all waiting for me. I can't wait to join my friends, to fill our sails with the friendly winds of the eternal ocean. And you know something else, I would like to see my old enemies there as well, the Dorias, the Cornaros and the Bifallis so that we can stand shoulder to shoulder together before our maker on Judgement Day!

Believe me, Koca Sinan, there is nothing in this long hard life that I haven't owned or experienced. Hundreds of lithe young things have shared my bed. There have been times when I have jettisoned chests of Ducats into the sea. I have been master of far flung lands, fleets of ships and the sea itself. I have also seen my wrists worn to the bone as a galley slave. The Sirocco has seared my skin and the sea spray burnt my eyes. I have ridden the fear streaked waves like a steed, galloping to the far reaches of the ocean. But now I feel it is time to abandon this worn shell and let the river of life ebb into the ocean."

He appeared to have aged as he stopped to catch his breath. A tear formed and then followed the contours of his face chiselled by the passing years only to disappear into his grizzled beard. He lifted his silver topped cane and waved it at the horizon and without looking at his friend began to speak again.

"Look over yonder, on top of that hill. Byzantine Giustiniani (Justinian) got his architects to bring the dome of the sky down to this earth. Am I asking too much, be it illegitimate Occhiali from Calabria or high and mighty *Kılıç* Ali Pasha and bearing in mind that sea comes between, to have you make me a small 'Divine Wisdom'[13] to cover the last mortal remains of this poor soul? And you of all people *Koca* Sinan, you have managed to lower the celestial dome time and time again, making you exalted amongst men. Don't look down on me, poor soul that I am and deny me my own small little Hagia Sophia?"

The two men fell into silence and surveyed the heights across the water. Eventually, the architect smoothed the dust in front of him, took out a small emerald topped dirk from his belt and started to draw in the dust.

"You would pass through the surrounding courtyard to the five domed entrance. The main support columns I would build on an north to south axis. Your tomb I would place in the garden behind the *mihrab*[14] and it would be carved from marble in the form of a galley."

The two men, deep in excited discourse, had not even noticed that day had passed into night.

13. Divine Wisdom: Hagia Sophia.

14. Mihrab: The niche inside the mosque that indicates the direction of Mecca.

The Creator's Evocation

The Grand Vizier Huseyin Pasha had eventually brought the sultan to the verge of uncontrollable rage. What with the delays to the completion of the mosque and the weeks of the Vizier's innuendo, each striking his head like a poison arrow, he had finally lost all control.

"I want my horse saddled and right now! Send word to the *Subaşı*.[15] Tell him to make sure that neither the head architect nor his men know of my intended visit to the site. And tell the *Bostancıbaşı* to bring his greasiest rope!"

Sultan Suleyman the Magnificent, ruler of the world, jumped to his feet. The courtiers jumped to their feet also and formed up in two rows, waiting in trepidation, their heads bowed there hands clasped together in supplication, praying for the storm of fury that was their sultan to pass them by untouched.

The sultan's noble white steed was waiting for him outside the audience chamber. It was as if every individual hair of the animal had been groomed. The saddle was decorated with solid gold. The bridle and bit were of silver and the mane had been plaited with silk cord at the end of each tassel was a precious jewel. An African groom crouched down to serve as the sultan's mounting block. He kicked aside the grooms holding the bridle causing the horse to shy, almost unseating the sultan in the process who grabbed for his turban as it was about to head groundward. Nobody had ever seen the sultan so enraged before.

The sultan galloped through the second great courtyard like a whirlwind and as he shot through the great ceremonial gate of *Babıhümayun* two troops of cavalry swept in beside him with

15. Subaşı: Chief of police.

one taking the vanguard and one taking up the rear of the galloping sultan. They tore through the square in front of Hagia Sophia like a gale scattering the clerics gathered there like dry leaves. There turned into the broad street known as *Divanyolu* without a break in their pace only to find the road was filled with worshippers coming from midday prayers, the cavalry troop now galloping ahead of the sultan, cracked their whips sending the people scuttling like startled partridges, running for refuge into the doorways and shops that lined the street. From there they watched mystified as their sultan thunder passed with his gold and white robes streaming behind him like so many banners.

The riders turned off the street and slowed as they entered the way that ran between the Beyazit mosque and the Grand Bazaar and that led to the contentious building site that had raised so much passion in the sultan.

Sultan Suleyman pulled back on his reins and started to try to regain his composure following their whirlwind ride from the Seraglio. He was breathing heavily. Remembering his exalted position he straightened his turban and wiped the sweat from his brow with the sleeve of his caftan. He then raised his head and looked at the stunning silhouette that the mosque presented to the world as it rose up from the *Kıble.*[16] For almost seven years he had been pouring his personal fortune into this project, something close to fifty million *Akçe*[17] had been spent. Here, the sultan thought, was the edifice that would reconcile him with his God. So why was that convert Sinan still fiddling around? Why was he continually delaying the inauguration, an event that would shake the earth around the world?

The court had been alive with gossip: There was no shortage of detractors for the Great Architect, they whispered that he had locked himself in this mosque, that he was smoking hashish and throwing parties for handsome young men, even that he was desecrating what would be one of Islam's masterpieces before it had even been consecrated! Now was the time for settling scores. If the Chief Architect really was a desecrator then he had to die! But then again, the sultan thought, the Sinan he thought he knew was a decent honest man, a devout man and how he had won his affection when he built the mosque dedicated to his sons' memory, the *Şehzade* mosque, it had gone some way towards atoning for his

16. Kıble: The direction of Mecca.

17. Akçe: Gold coin.

sadness for the son, Mustafa, whom he had needlessly strangled, just because of the intrigues of the Sultana Hurrem, and then there was his son Mehmed who could not bear life without his murdered brother. Even if he conquered the whole world he would never win Allah's forgiveness but at least Sinan had given him a chance to find a little grace, he would build the almighty a temple that would far outshine the Byzantine's Hagia Sophia.

The masons who were working high up on the façade could hardly conceal their surprise when they caught sight of the sultan, his face crimson with rage. The painters' brushes froze in their hands, the masons' hammers remained hovering in the air, the smiths' forges cooled, the labourers' loads remained motionless in their hods and everybody waited to see what would happen next. The Grand Vizier, who had caught up with the Sultan, stood breathless next to him at the entrance to the mosque. Behind them stood the *Bostancıbaşı*, like an angel of death with his greased cord in his hand. The sultan gave them a glance to indicate that they were to wait for him there and he slipped into the mosque. The afternoon sun filtered through the stain glass commissioned from *Sarhoş*[18] Ibrahim that was sited above the *mihrab*. The light was fractured into thousands of tones of colour that danced on the marble floor like a hymn to the glory of God. Great Sinan sat seated alone on a stool in the middle of the space. Beside him was a water pipe he sucked on the mouthpiece that he held to his lips.

The sultan broke out in a cold sweat. His heart became constricted. He did not want to believe it but everything he heard appeared to be true. As he was about to turn and summon the executioner he stayed his decision. The noise that Sinan was making with the pipe echoed around the domed edifice like divine music, like the waves in an ocean of eternity. The strangest thing was that there was neither smoke, nor was their tobacco nor fire in the pipe's bowl. The ruler of the world needed to watch no longer. He summoned the executioner with a wave of his hand. The executioner, his greased cord held in both hands, quietly approached. The sultan whispered a command. The Architect Sinan who, up until that moment, had given no indication that he did not think he was alone, took the pipe from his mouth and spoke without turning his head.

"My sultan, you know I would happily sacrifice my life for you. But all I ask of you is that you allow me, your humble servant,

18. Sarhoş: ecstatic.

one or two more days of existence so that I can complete the Sulemaniye mosque to the highest level of purity so that Allah's evocation can ring out loud and true. I am going to deliver you a temple the like of which the world has never seen before, so that the world hears your glory and your fame ascends to the seventh heaven. If I could put it into words it would sound like this:

> The domes of your mosque are like the swell adorning the surface of the open seas. As for the mighty central dome, it is like a representation of the heavens drawn in gold. This great dome and the four minarets are like our dear Prophet and his four closest companions. The windows are of embroidered coloured glass, matchless in their beauty, like the ever-changing colours on the wings of the angel Gabriel or like the lustrous colours of the garden of Eden. All can only marvel at the rainbow colours of the glass changing, chameleon-like, with the rays of the sun.[19]

Allow me, my sultan , to carry out the final acoustic adjustments of your dome so that I can deliver your mosque to you as a place where the heavens may descend to earth.

Sultan Suleyman stood, mouth ajar, staring at the great architect as he waited, erect, in front of the *mihrab* with speckles of colour pouring down on him from the stained glass above, and could think of not a word to say. Eventually, he pulled himself away and turned his back. He gave the order while trying to conceal the tears welling up in his eyes:

"Complete your work, Chief Architect! Your work is blessed! You name will be cherished, both in this world and in the next! You are clearly one Allah's servants!" As much as the sultan tried to make his words sound hard and authoritative there was no disguising the affection and love that they carried.

The executioner dispatched the Grand Vizier right there and then, at the entrance to the mosque. As the sultan walked towards his horse, he heard the sound of the Great Architect recommence his work. He paused and was overwhelmed by a desire to kneel down and bow his head. He resisted this urge and carried on walking purposefully toward his horse.

The guard following two paces behind could have sworn he heard the sultan say: 'It is as though it were the final day and the Seraphim are calling all humanity to stand before their maker'. But he could have been mistaken.

19. Taken from Mimar Sinan's Tezkiretü'l Bünyan (An Account of His Works).

A Watery Grave

Sultan Ibrahim wearing majestic red robes and a regal white turban walked, with his hands behind his back, from the inner court towards the Baghdad pavilion. His Grand Vizier followed, a discrete few paces behind, and was animatedly imparting something of great importance but the Sultan was clearly not listening to a word. Further behind, a hand picked platoon of the Imperial guard, matched their every step.

The look in the sultan's eyes could not, by any stretch of the imagination, be called normal. He continued to walk, occasionally stroking his pearl adorned beard, as though he might be paying attention to what his Vizier had to say. However, his mind was firmly on the previous night and his shameful impotence while lying with a Circassian beauty called Dilhayat; indeed, Dilhayat was not just any beauty she was without doubt the most beautiful woman in the whole Harem.

The night before that the same thing had happened, that time with a dusky beauty with almond eyes called Gulistan. He had caught his breath when they brought her to him dressed in pink silk. He told the head eunuch that Gulistan was to remain with him for the whole night. But, despite her body being as though carved from ivory and her skin smelling of every perfume the Orient could offer, not to mention the fact that she excelled in the art of love, she failed to stir 'Mad Ibrahim' one iota.

There was something horribly not right in all of this. Here was the descendant of Mehmed the Conqueror and Sultan Yavuz, here was the Sultan Ibrahim Khan from the blessed Ottoman dynasty and yet he had been betrayed! Someone had cast a spell on him! After having lived for so many years in the hellish confinement of the *kafes*[20] nobody could take from him now what was rightfully his. This he would never allow! He was convinced that he had been treacherously betrayed and the only punishment for that was death! He would extract every last drop of revenge from those who had taken advantage of him and had been so ungrateful to their benefactor.

After they had entered the Baghdad pavilion the sultan turned his crazed gaze on the terrified and cowering Vizier. The sultan stood erect and gave his decree:

"You shall have every one of my concubines and hand-maidens in the Harem killed forthwith! I want a new Harem established right away, with the most beautiful maidens taken from every corner of the empire. Oh yes, there is one other thing, the palace doctor who is supposed prepare my virility potions, have his head removed this instant. His charlatan head shall be nailed to the door of the Harem and not removed until the new concubines arrive!"

The vizier had difficulty taking in the horror of these commands and remained rooted to the spot, but so wild was the look in the sultan's eyes that something told him that if he did not start to carry these orders right away he would feel the greased cord of the executioner around his own neck too.

The vizier bowed low and saying: "As you command my sovereign" he left the pavilion and conveyed the decree to the Seraglio commander and told him to carry out the orders as soon as possible.

The evening meal in the Harem had been eaten and cleared away. Some of the concubines sang to the accompaniment of string instruments while some rose from the floor to dance to the poignant melodies. Other sat by the windows, entranced by the lights of the city below which they viewed through the trellis shutters. The keeper of the household busied herself, she kept an account of which of the concubines were in the sultan's favour and counted the days for those who were with child.

When they heard the doors of the Harem crashing open nobody had an inkling of what was to befall them. Quickly the Harem was full of soldiers who roughly man-handled the women and started dragging them out of the place.

20. Kafes: The guarded apartments in the palace where the heirs to the throne were confined.

The head eunuch let out a wail and then cried out: " How dare you violate the sultan's Harem!" In answer, the Seraglio commander stepped forward and brought down his broad sword on the unfortunate's head, splitting it open like a ripe water melon. The terrified screams of the women could be heard in every corner of the Seraglio. Some were dragged out by their hair others like trussed animals. They were thrown on top each other in carts waiting in the outer court. Two hundred and ninety nine of the most beautiful women in the world, but now totally wretched as they started out on their doomed journey. The carts halted at the point on the coast called *Sarayburnu* where they were brutally thrown onto the deck of a naval ship moored to the pier. Soldiers boarded and started to put the women into sacks weighted with stones. Their heart rending cries for mercy fell on deaf ears. Their executioners were only concerned about completing their orders and avoiding reprimand, they quickly tied the sacks and threw their victims, one by one, into the deep dark swirling waters of the Bosphorus.

Dilhayat and Gulistan, made no struggle and uttered not a sound but stood proudly erect waiting their turn. They had both resigned themselves to their fate and saw no point in attempting to cling on to life. When their turn came they stepped forward offering no resistance and to the surprise of their executioners took hold of their sacks and stepped into them, pulling them up as if they were trying a new dress. The soldiers only hesitated for a second, they tied up the mouths of the sacks and threw them into the dark swirling waters along with the rest of them.

The sultan, 'Mad Ibrahim', stood on a terrace of the *Topkapı* Seraglio that overlooked the Bosphorus, observing the terrible events below. He smiled to himself when he saw the ship's lights twinkle as they disappeared from view. They must have finished their work, he thought. The traitors had met their end! Now a completely new Harem awaited him. Friend and foe, they would all understand him now! The spell casters had been routed! Soon the Harem would be full of the sound rocking cribs and nursery rhymes.

He put his hands behind his back and walked to the corner. He paused by the garden's decorative pool. He watched the multi-coloured fish swimming in its depths. He then took a handful of pearls from his pocket and started to cast them in the pool one by one. The small fished disturbed by the splashing pearls shot around the pool creating patterns that began to form into a vision in the deranged sultan's mind. Two hundred and ninety nine beautiful women, their hair like a dance of death in the currents, stared back at him from their watery grave.

Have All My Brothers Strangled!

For two days the snowstorm continued unabated leaving Constantiniye covered in a blanket of snow. The Grand Mufti, Bostanzade Efendi, despite the freezing cold, paced up down on the Seraglio's exposed north terrace. The day before the bitterly cold weather had descended upon the city from the north, The Sultan Murad-i Salis (Murad III) had started coughing up blood, due, it was supposed, to the excess of wine he had consumed during his dinner and he had been lying on his death bed ever since.

The Grand Mufti turned the events of the last few days over in his mind: 'Anyone who dispatches five innocent souls of his own blood to the executioner, without batting an eyelid, is not going to let go of life that easily, God must have something planned!' He looked up and saw the doors to the Sultan's bed chamber thrown open. He saw the candle-lit outline of the Grand Vizier gazing out into the night. When he caught sight of the Grand Mufti through the flurries of snow he motioned for him to come while calling out:

"Come your excellency the Grand Mufti, our master the sultan has given up his spirit!"

The Grand Vizier cleared his throat before addressing the highest officials of the state gathered in the council chamber. He read from the decree that he had drafted:

"As you are all undoubtedly aware, of the one hundred and two children the late sultan sired, there are alive at this moment, twenty seven daughters and twenty sons. Furthermore, the late sultan, may his soul be blessed, sent his eldest son, Prince Mehmed, to govern the principality of Manisa. The other offspring have remained here in the palace. Having given it our due consideration, our opinion is that the succession should pass directly to Prince Mehmed. Therefore a messenger should be sent immediately to summon him to Constantiniye to take his place on the throne. Furthermore, until his arrival here, the death of the late sultan should not be publicly announced."

It took eleven days for the message to be delivered and for the new sultan to arrive in Constantiniye. He was presented with the sword of the Exalted Caliph Osman and then assisted in having it bound to his waist. The young sultan ascended to the throne as Mehmed III. In the afternoon he attended the celebrations held in front of the Gate of Felicity in honour of the occasion. Before he sat down for dinner he summoned the oldest of his brothers, Mustafa, Bayezid, Osman and Abdullah. When they arrived before him they each kissed his hand in a sign of respect and allegiance. He immediately won them over by saying he would arrange for their circumcision ceremonies to take place immediately, the last rite of passage into manhood. At eleven years, the oldest of them, Mustafa, stepped forward and said:

"May Allah bless you and protect you for us and all your people, our exalted brother!" He then led the way by prostrating himself before his brother and kissing the hem of his robe. He then escorted his brothers back to their quarters.

Mustafa knew that his young brothers had no idea of what would befall them, but he was well aware of what fate held in store for all of them the moment their father died. His tutor, Nevi, had attempted not to dwell on the Law of Succession when teaching Ottoman history. Devised by his great grandfather Mehmed Khan, it attempted to avoid fraternal rivalry for the throne by removing all rivals, apart from the appointed one. Every succeeding sultan had bowed to this law written, as it was, in the blood of their brothers. There was no escaping the fact, the same fate awaited him and his brothers. In the two weeks that had elapsed since his father died, Mustafa's sleep was punctuated with nightmares of death. He thanked God each morning when he saw the first rays of dawn. He mentioned his fears to his tutor, in fact he penned a couplet to voice the injustice of his destiny:

With knowledge of what is written by fate,
Who could broach a smile in this rosy state.

After paying their respects to their brother, the new sultan, his mind was only plagued further by these dark thoughts. He lay tossing and turning in his bed in the section of the Harem reserved for the young princes. How was it, that even though it had not been his decision to enter this world, he would have no say about when he would leave it? How was he going to die? When he saw the executioner before him, would he be able to control his fear? But then again, perhaps things would change, perhaps this heart-ache was all in vain, after all, his brother, the sultan, had called for him and his brothers to come to him. He had smiled at them and promised them a splendid circumcision ceremony. He had raised no objection nor looked ill at ease when they made obeisance to him.

He looked over at his younger brothers with whom he shared the room. They were all fast asleep, the sleep of the innocent as though angels looked over them. No, he thought, perhaps death was a long way off. There would be many more happy days. They would hunt wild geese again in the Belgrade Forest, they would have days of endless pleasure sailing on the royal caique, and at the end of those days watch the sun set over the Bosphorus, each one of these equal to a life time. With that in his mind, thoughts of death slipped over the horizon and Mustafa surrendered himself to sleep.

The new sultan had watched carefully as his younger brothers trooped off to their beds and then called for his secretary and told him to summon his council forthwith. The command flew around the passages and courtyards of the Seraglio:

'The viziers, clerics and all officials of state are summoned to the sultan's council!'

Less than half an hour later the Sultan's council had gathered in the council chamber. There was no doubt in anyone's mind what the reason for this was. They would, that night, all be accomplices in condemning to death nineteen young lives. The youngest still at their mother's breasts, the oldest without as much as down upon their chins.

The grand Mufti raised his hand for silence. The new sultan whom history would remember as Mehmed III, rubbed his hands together and then stroked his beard before addressing the chamber.

"My lords, we have been called to the throne as the sole ruler of the Ottoman possessions and as the Caliph, the shadow of the creator on earth, and also as the sultan of three worlds. To comply with the Law of Succession created by my illustrious forefather, Sultan Mehmed Khan the Conqueror, and presented to his subjects for the eternal maintenance of the state, the protection of the faith and for the welfare of all, I seek both divine assistance and yours, for the decision we will take here tonight. Esteemed Grand Mufti, where is your decree? Read it out loud in a clear voice for our honoured gathering."

The ageing limbs and joints of the Grand Mufti, Bostanzade Efendi, made it quite a struggle for him to rise to his feet. He brought his hand to his mouth to conceal a discreet belch before muttering, 'excuse me'. And then, in a screeching voice reminiscent of a badly played fiddle, he read out the decree:

"May the Lord provide for our Sultan!"

The whole chamber gave the response as one voice 'Amen!'

"May the gates of Paradise be opened wide for the deceased, Murad Khan, so that he may embrace the life eternal!"

"Amen!"

"Our exalted Sultan, the Ottoman throne is a lofty pinnacle, the whole world's eyes are upon it. However, your brothers here now are like angels but as they grow their innocence could be exploited by those within and those without to instigate intrigue and insurrection so that your divine majesty could be threatened or even overthrown. Furthermore, the very fabric of the state could be endangered, our faith under attack and our enemies could even enter this our sacred motherland.

For these reasons it is imperative that the princes be dispatched this very night! May we commend their soles to God. In the name of God the merciful, the compassionate. Praise be to God, the lord of the worlds!"

The Grand Mufti's heart was breaking as he read these words. But he had to consider first his life and those of his loved ones. Had he refused this duty there would have been no further reason for the greased cord not to have been slipped over his head, his belongings confiscated and his loved ones scattered and the fire put out in the family hearth. His hands were tied, there was nothing else he could do.

"Lord have mercy upon us!" He uttered and then started leading the prayers.

When the prayers were concluded, the sultan announced in a commanding voice that he reluctantly concurred with the Grand Mufti's decree.

"We are the sword of the faith and the shield of the state. There is nothing we desire for ourselves. Our family or our sentiments can never come before our duty to the state. The Grand Mufti's decree must be carried out to the letter. Lord High Executioner take your tongueless accomplices with you and strangle all my brothers! Their funerals will take place tomorrow morning after prayers and they will be interred in my father, Murad III's, tomb at Hagia Sophia."

Just as the Lord High Executioner was saying 'your word is my command, my sovereign' and kissing the hem of the sultan's robe, the Grand Mufti whispered something into the sultan's ear. He listened intently to what the Grand Mufti had to say and gestured to the executioner to remain where he was, he then modified the executioner's orders.

"First you will go to the women's quarters of the Harem and wake the Head Eunuch. I am told that there are seven concubines pregnant with my siblings, there is some suspicion that there might even be ten, so let's not take any chances. Get the Eunuch to identify these women and have them put into weighted sacks. They should then be thrown into the sea at Seraglio Point. This should be dealt with first before you carry out my previous orders."

This time the grim faced executioner just nodded before kissing the hem of the Sultan's robe before hurrying from the chamber.

Shortly before midnight, the Lord High Executioner, with his four villainous and mute assistants beside him, burst through the doors of the Harem. Outside the weather had deteriorated and there was now almost a blizzard blowing up. The head eunuch was woken by the Harem guards. At first the giant of a Nubian swore at the guards but then quickly realised the gravity of the situation. He hurriedly pulled on his robe and hastily made his way to where the agitated executioner and his henchmen waited. When he saw who had so rudely dragged him from his slumbers his mouth dropped wide in horror and the candle he held in his hand began to tremble. The executioner repeated the sultan's command in a hurried rasp. The Eunuch started nodding his head and produced the Harem register from one of the copious pockets of his robe. He licked his finger and, holding the black book close to his eyes, started flicking through the pages murmuring to himself. He had been joined by a tall black woman, the senior housekeeper, Sati Kalfa, who stood beside him like a bird of death. With a nod of his head he gave her a quiet order and she left. Mere minutes passed before she returned pushing ten sleepy, confused and beautiful pregnant women in front of her. Before they even understood what was happening these unfortunates were roughly bound by the four mutes and bundled outside.

Half an hour later one of his majesty's galleys cast off from Seraglio Point to row the short distance to middle of the Bosphorus where they would unload, into the deep murky waters, their cargo of the damned.

While this was happening the executioner and his henchmen had already started the second part of their dreadful command. They quietly slipped into the princes' quarters in the Harem. When Mustafa saw the shadows approaching he immediately realised that his worst nightmares were about to come true. He sat up straight in his bed surprising the assassins who had just entered the room. Mustafa held up his hand and spoke in a whisper.

"My Lords, I am not going to resist you I am aware of what the sultan must do, but at least allow me to say my prayers before you act."

The Lord High Executioner had to restrain his deaf and dumb galloglasses who had not heard the prince. He too spoke in a whisper and told the prince that he would not be hindered in his devotions. Mustafa then quietly woke up the eldest of his siblings, Osman, Bayezid and Abdullah and whispered to them what was to befall them. When they heard of their terrible fate they started to tremble uncontrollably but Mustafa by his example and soothing words managed to calm them. He raised them from their beds and got them to stand next to him in a row facing East. They then started their prayers. Meanwhile, the executioner had motioned to his henchmen to go behind the small princes and on his command they threw their greased cords around the children's necks and strangled them. Mustafa could only manage to recite '*La ilaha il...*' before his life was snuffed out. From the others not a word escaped their lips.

The executioners with cold precision entered the next room where the even younger princes lay, Selim, Cihangir, Abdurrahman and Hasan. Their short lives finished for them while they were still in their sleep. However, the noise had woken up the princes in the adjoining room, Ahmed, Yakub, Yusuf, Huseyin and Korkut who all now sat up in bed. They did not understand until it was too late that the black deathly shadows entering their room signified their end.

The youngest of the princes were still babes and were being breast fed in the nursery when the assassins threw back the door. Ali, Ishak, Omer, Alaadin and Davud understood nothing but started to cry when their wet-nurses started to resist. The knives they pulled out in an attempt to protect their charges were buried into their own hearts as they screamed out 'Have mercy on these innocents!'. They fell beside the cradles in which their now crying charges lay. These professional murderers who had so skilfully dispatched their brothers had never strangled a baby before and had difficulty at first , the cords were too thick and cumbersome. But within five minutes the last of the brothers was dead and, as with all the others, the executioner made a final check to see that they no longer lived. He was more than satisfied with the job he had done. Now he could send a secret messenger back to his village in Serbia from where he had been indentured so many years before. His father was the bell-ringer in the village and after hearing how his son had despatched nineteen of the sultan's male heirs he would invite the messenger to his house and, after feeding and giving him plenty to drink, would strangle him in his sleep.

> ...after the executioners had carried out their fateful deed, the corpses were scrupulously washed and prepared for burial by those appointed. They were then wrapped in their shrouds and placed in their coffins bearing the royal arms. Each coffin was borne by four axemen and four gatekeepers assisted by pages and heralds they were carried from the palace through the Gate of Felicity.
>
> All the dignitaries of state joined the cortege as it passed in front of the Matbah-Amire gate arriving at the Helvahane gate where the coffins were placed on wooden biers. The Grand Mufti led the gathered in prayers and performed the funeral rites for each one separately.
>
> The weeping that accompanied the loss of these innocent souls rose to the heavens like sweet smoke. No heart was spared the pain this burning caused. With eyes wet with tears and tongues silent they bore those frail bodies to the foot of their father's tomb where they were interred.

The date of the martyrdom of these noble Ottoman princes was the 17th day of the fifth month 1003 (Hijre) or (28th January 1595).[21]

21. Contemporary account: Tarihi Selanki, Selanikli Mustafa Efendi, Vol.II, pages 435-436 quoted from Fratrocide in the Ottoman State by Dr. Mehmet Akman, Eren Yayınları, Istanbul 1997.

Sultaness of The East, Empress of The West

The empress stood by the window of the *Salon des Nobles* in Versailles and took her first gentle sip of linden tea before turning to her secretary and dictating the details of the ball she was organising to commemorate Napoleon's victory at Austerlitz.

"Make sure that each of the gold napkin rings engraved with the letter 'N' are facing upward. I do not want as much as a millimetre error in the distance between the cutlery. If there is as much as a speck of dust on the crystal glasses the culprit will be sent to the guillotine!"

She was distracted by a knock at the door. She put down her cup and saucer and picked up a fan lying on the escritoire and fanned herself petulantly for a moment before calling out in an imperious tone, 'entrez!'. The door was slowly opened and then closed by a footman to let in the chamberlain who walked slowly toward the empress holding a silver tray in both hands. She raised one eyebrow at the stiff-backed lackey and said:

"You must have had a very important reason!"

"Pardon me your highness, but we received this letter addressed to you a short while ago through a special messenger from our embassy in Constantinople; it has 'Top Secret' and 'Most Urgent' written on it and bears the sultan's arms."

Although burning up with curiosity, she feigned disinterest and nodded for the chamberlain to bring her the letter. She could not maintain her role for long, for as she opened the letter she thought she was going to burst with excitement. When she read the first lines she could control herself no longer and let out a small shriek and jumped in the air.

"Aimée? Aimée de Rivery? Could it really be you?" She declared aloud and then started to read from the letter:

My Dearest Josephine,

It seems like a lifetime ago, does it not? You recall our childhood in Martinique and how we would collect shrimps and shells together on the beach? How we would laugh! All our days were filled with running, climbing trees and collecting coconuts, you remember the taste of fresh coconut milk? We were cousins, but we were inseparable, more like two sisters really. You remember how our mothers would drill us on how, with a good education, we would find well-placed husbands for ourselves and spend a life in the lap of wealth and happiness? As you recall that was why we were both sent to boarding school in France. We were inseparable until the moment when we finished our schooling in Nantes and I was to be sent back to Martinique.

I am still reminded of that sadness, particularly as when I boarded that ship from the quay in Nantes bound for Martinique, it was a moment that would also mark the end of my childhood too. It was only a day after we set sail from France when we were set upon by pirates in the middle of the night. They attacked and boarded our ship and took the survivors including myself captive. After a number of days we arrived in Algiers. I was taken to the slave market, where I saw there were many other young women of different nationalities in the same sorry state. We were examined like horses by the most hideous looking men. They squeezed our thighs, opened our mouths to examine our teeth and then started bargaining for us with the slave master. But my destiny was not to be sold to the highest bidder, instead fate would take me to the most celebrated palace of the whole Orient.

There was a commotion in the market and we understood that it was to be visited by a very important dignitary. I later learnt that he was the Governor-General of Algiers. He was a very serious and grave looking man but it was he who saved me from that terrible fate. He gave some orders and immediately I was taken from that place and began to be treated with far greater respect; within days I was on a ship bound for Constantinople. During the voyage I thought of you constantly and reminisced about the innocence of our happy childhood together. When I eventually saw Constantinople, emerging out of the morning mist, I was totally captivated. It was a magical panorama with skylines adorned with domes and minarets.

As soon as we landed I was taken to the Harem of the Seraglio. I was allowed to rest for a few days to recover from my ordeal. I decided that if I were to survive I shouldn't put up a struggle and acquiesce. I did not resist when I was told that I was to be taken before the sultan for a 'face viewing'. Before this I was taken for my first visit to a Turkish bath. I marvelled at the way the domed ceiling seemed have a thousand eyes looking down at you. I was washed and prepared with minute attention to detail. I was then dressed in brightly coloured silk clothes and small red shoes decorated with pompoms. I was taken before the sultan and when he removed my veil and looked at me with those haughty eagle eyes, I knew that I was his.

To explain how I shared him with hundreds of other women and the endless intrigues of Seraglio life would fill countless pages. We still love each other intensely and he made me his 'first wife' and I have given him beautiful children. And, most precious of all, my son Mahmud is heir to the throne. He is a wise ruler and has introduced a programme of reforms that were long overdue. He is the first sultan to have had the will and determination to disband the corps of Janissaries whose power and influence was so great that they could topple viziers and even sultans.

Dearest Josephine, I really write to you because I wished to tell you that I am seriously ill. I have learnt from the French Ambassador's wife that your adventures have been no less dramatic than my own. I understand you lost your first husband, Alexandre de Beauharnais, to the Guillotine during the Reign of Terror and that you yourself came within a whisker of loosing your own head. She told me how, and with a great love, you married the new conqueror of Europe, Napoleon Bonaparte and how you have become the Empress of the West.

As I write to you, I am about to be measured for my shroud, but as I contemplate my own death, I think of the strange game fate played on those two small Creole girls. For one, from a slave market to a sultaness and for the other, from the guillotine to an empress! No small achievement when you think about it!

I embrace you with all my love and till we meet again in another life.

Aimée (Valide Nakşidil Sultan)

Paradise Beneath The Glaze

Who knows how many times before this the apprentice's eyes had lit up in wonder when he had seen the tiles first appear from the kiln. After gazing at these tiny miracles spellbound for quite some time he turned to the master craftsman, who was sitting in a corner carefully painting new glaze designs with a sable brush, and spoke to him still with the light of wonder in his eyes and the miracle of verse on his tongue:

How do you create such beauty, master,
Has the light of God fallen upon you?
How did you squeeze in these visions of paradise,
On the simple clay fired in that heat so blue?
How from the tip of your brush,
Did these gardens of Eden appear?
And who are you master,
To capture them beneath a glaze so hard and clear?
Are you as exalted as your name?
Or are you a mystic arrayed as a sage?

The master looked up from his work and smiled indulgently at his young apprentice:

No need for exaggeration, young man,
The product of my hands was passed down to me,
From China and India and also Iran,
And here in Iznik it took root and we do toil,
pouring the light of my poor soul,
Over this pungent and ardent clay soil.

From the sky we got azure,
Nature gave us its green,
The yellow sun its allure,
And red from flames, ever so rare,
So that I mixed them up, one to one,
And then separated them with a single hair.

I made the world anew with flowers,
My eternal carnations speak their verse,
In competition with the 'One' I wasted no hours,
And so my tulips and lilies sing their praises,
The word of the creator in white and blue,
On the walls of holy places in fresh vibrant glazes.
On my dishes, vases and tiles I drew
The promised heaven
Bringing it into the world anew.
I never once could be accused
Of portraying a mortal sole,
Except, of course, for those in nature so imbued.

The apprentice was in awe of his master's words but something troubled him still.

Master, you have spoken well,
May I always be in your debt,
My eyes sometimes see an idolater's hell,
But my heart tells me it is but angels yet.

The master warmed to his apprentice's words:

Well done, my boy, well done,
You have studied well!
But make no hasty conclusion!
What you see are three thousand year motifs,
Coming down to us from China, India and the near East,
And in Iznik, refined as a product of our beliefs.

The master called the apprentice over to observe him as he explained:

This dragon form,
Like smothered thunder,

Is a white cloud at dawn,
It is the symbol of eternity.

The forms you see as triple cross eyes
Are the stones of Cintamani,
Have no fear,
For the eyes are the eyes of wisdom.
And the circles divided in the middle clear,
Are like the dervish's dance,
Which are called Tai-Chi in China,
Or Ying and Yang perchance,
Representing the duality of earth.
Night and day,
Better and worse,
Or the male and female,
As we add to our collective knowledge,
From the flux of our art we remove the veil,
And thus elevating the observer
To a higher level.

We have no fear of the new,
As everything that is, is from the creator.
On our baked clay we do what we can do,
Nature's limitless palette,
Or the Creator's flora and fauna.

A sip of water,
And a morsel of bread is all we desire.
Our heart gives no quarter,
For the love of material, property or wealth.
It matters not that we live in a cloud,
Whither or thither,
Because to draw the Creator's universe of love we are truly
avowed.

Bathhouse Besime

The young woman gently tapped twice on the heavy mahogany door before pushing it open and entering the *directeur*'s office. The dim and gloomy light hardly revealed the depths of the expansive room and this along with the high ceiling was an indication of some former grandeur. The large windows were hung with heavy and faded red velvet curtains that only allowed a sliver of daylight to enter the room. The *directeur* was bent over his Louis XV bureau, he continued to scribble without raising his head as he addressed his secretary.

"Very good, Georgette, I assume everything is in order."

"Monsieur *le directeur*, I have done as you instructed and have escorted your guests to the waiting room. Two men and three women, quite ordinary in appearance, I must say. The bank's legal advisor, Monsieur Batchelet, has looked over the documents bearing the Justice Ministry seal and indicated everything is as it should be. He is waiting with them."

The *directeur*, put down his pen, pushed his chair back and stood up. He adjusted his tie and discretely groomed his moustache.

"*Bon*, let's us go and settle this affair, Georgette. And, talking of which, I will dine tonight with Mademoiselle Denise at *L'Arrosée* in Saint Germain. Please can you make sure I have my usual table and, it goes without saying, what you have to say to Madam Chapus should she call."

The Banque Ottoman had once been a grand building on Rue Meyerbeer, one of Paris's most eminent thoroughfares, but now, as the *directeur* was constantly reminded, even the furniture was of another age. The centre of the waiting room was dominated by a massive walnut table around which sat his five guests. They rose to their feet as he entered the room. Monsieur Batchelet introduced the guests to the *directeur.*

"*Mesdames et Messieurs*, may I introduce the *directeur* of the Banque Ottoman, Monsieur André Chapus. And Monsieur Chapus may I introduce their majesties, the Princesses and Princes who are the legitimate heirs to the Ottoman legacy. I have examined the documents pertinent to this claim, each of which has been authenticated by the ministry, and I can verify that there is no legal impediment why the wishes of the late Valide Sultan, the Queen Mother, cannot be enacted."

The *directeur* smiled and gestured to the chairs. He waited for them to sit down before sitting down himself. He re-arranged the documents that the legal advisor had placed in front of him. He then sat back put his hands together and addressed his guests.

"*D'accord*, if you permit me I will just summarise the situation. On June 5th 1887, the Valide Sultan summoned the manager of the Ottoman Bank in Istanbul, M. Gilbert Benoir, to the palace. He went accompanied by our company's lawyer M. Andon. Together they drew up and witnessed a will for the Valide Sultan. The only stipulation of the will was that a small strongbox be handed over to the bank for safe keeping with the further instructions that on the first day of 2000 the strongbox and its contents be delivered to her then living legitimate heirs.

As we are all aware a great deal has changed in the time that has elapsed and to cite the course of historical events at this juncture would not be of any particular use. Suffice to say, as you most probably are aware, the Ottoman Bank is in the process of being acquired by a Turkish financial group. The formalities are close to completion. We are therefore trying to settle our customers' business and close the accounts of those not wishing to continue under new management, prior to the takeover being formalised. In consultation with our colleagues in the Ministry of Justice, it has therefore been decided to hand over the contents of the bank safe-deposit box a short time before the actual stipulated date; this could be considered a *force majeur* provision and is not governed by any of the international agreements concerning the assets of the former Ottoman state following the founding of the Turkish Republic in 1923, added to which this is considered to be both a private account and provision."

The *directeur* paused, looked at each of the beneficiaries in turn and then smiling, softly clapped his hands together. "Now let us proceed to the vault where we can carry out the wishes of the late Valide Sultan."

The *directeur* ushered them to the door and then led them down the broad marble staircase. The musty damp air gave each of them a frisson of foreboding as they descended into the bowels of the building. The guard in the vault jumped to his feet when he saw the *directeur* and his party approach. The *directeur* instructed him to open the vault door. They entered the vault together and the *directeur* took a key from his pocket and put it into one of the key holes of safety-deposit box number 119, he nodded at M. Bachelet who took out another apparently identical key and put it into the other hole, they both turned their keys at the same time and opened the door of the strongbox. They stepped back and gestured for the guard to remove the heavy steel box.

"Please follow the guard, he will take you to the viewing room and then leave you alone. There you will be able to examine the contents of the box in privacy. When you have completed your examination you can ring for the guard and then if you come to my office again I will ask you to sign the release document. There are a few other minor formalities we must take care of and then you are free to leave with your inheritance."

After the guard had left them, one of the men leapt forward and lifting the top off the safe-deposit box he slowly raised the square lid of the small strongbox nestling inside. The others were soon quickly by his side. Filling the interior of the box was a bundle wrapped in ageing red velvet. The taller of the men who had a bushy moustache gently lifted the bundle from the box. They now could see that it was, in fact, not a bundle at all but a bag with a draw string mouth. They all looked into the box to see if there was anything else. But all they could see was the accumulation of over a hundred years of red dust from the decaying velvet. The man with the bushy moustache stood up and raised his eyebrows at the others and started to undo the drawstring. He pulled out a roll of paper, he then shook the bag and that was all the bag seemed to contain. He then turned the bag upside down and shook it angrily. From the depths of the bag a small boxwood comb and a few coins fell on the table. All four looked down at the table in disbelief. Again it was the man with the bushy moustache who showed the first reaction.

"And that's it, dear cousins! There, before your very eyes, is the spectacular inheritance of 'Her Glorious Majesty Valide Sultan', something that has had us jumping around like fleas on a dog since we first heard of it! Are you not impressed? Does it not bitterly remind you of how we have all gone short just to pay the exorbitant lawyers' fees to get us to this point? Anyone have any suggestions about what we do now?"

Two of the women both let out a sob. The men both voiced their anger in low growls and turned to the sympathy of nicotine to soothe their anger by lighting up cigarettes. One of the women, who had stood back while her cousins had become so elated and deflated in such quick succession, now stepped forward. She picked up the roll of papers and, as she did so, a pink envelope bearing the Valide Sultan's seal slipped from the roll and landed on the table. All their eyes were on the envelope, the woman put down the roll of papers and picked up the envelope instead. The man with the bushy moustache snatched it from her hand before, as an afterthought, glancing at her as if seeking some kind of permission. But his eyes did not linger either on her still outstretched hand nor on her face as he held the envelope up to the light turning it around to examine it.

"What's this then? Well done Mihriban! Perhaps we did react a little prematurely! Who knows, maybe our great grand-mother did leave us something after all! Somebody give me something to open the envelope with. Yes, that will do, we don't want to damage the contents, do we? Maybe she has left us details of a secret bank account? That's it, it's some kind of letter and what has she written here, I wonder? Let me see if I can still read the old script:

> My precious children,
>
> I will know none of you. And perhaps when you read this you will sneer at me when you realise that this is all there is by way of inheritance of her highness the Valide Sultan. However, if only one of you reads these memories which I have written down on these modest sheets of paper, they will have won my heart, and if they were to say a prayer in my memory who knows what riches they might receive from on high.
>
> You must be aware that wealth, money, possessions, they are all a deceit. When I was first noticed in the street by the Sultan Mahmud II and taken to the palace, all I had in the world was the boxwood

comb and the few copper coins that you have found in the bag. What can we do when we are merely the will of God and who could have predicted that the bathhouse gypsy girl Besime, from the Çemberlitaş Hamamı, would one day become the wife and favourite of the Sultan Mahmud Kahn and be the mother of his lion of a son, Sultan Abdulaziz. I became the possessor of uncountable riches, but be aware, just as when we came into the world, when we leave it also we have nothing, nothing but the sheet we are wrapped in. Search carefully amongst the lines I have written and you will find what I have left you my children! By the time you read this my body will have long since become one with the earth, but all I ask from you is a prayer, a prayer for the soul of your great grand-mother...

...and so on, and so on, and so on. So there it is, your majesty the Valide Sultan, instead of inheriting a fortune we get your invaluable wisdom! Now, try and spend that if you will! I have a sparkling suggestion, we men shall share the copper coins between us and you ladies can have the boxwood comb and these crumpled sheets, what do you say to that! Now let's get out of this mouldy basement, I am getting claustrophobic, let's go and see if the *directeur* has any suggestions to add to this!"

The two men, both with cigarettes in their mouths and hands in their pockets, slouched out of the room. Two of women looked at each other, shrugged their shoulders and followed the men. The third woman, Mihriban, remained where she was. When the others had mounted the stairs she went back to where their great grand-mother's belongings still lay on the table. She put the roll of papers, the copper coins and the comb back into the velvet bag and pulled the string tight. She picked up the letter and started reading it but within a few phrases her eyes began to well up. She carefully folded the letter and put it into the pink envelope, paused and then put it in her pocket. She went to the door, turned and gave the room a last look and quickly followed in the footsteps of her cousins.

M. Chapus was immediately made to realise that there was not the same level of excitement and anticipation amongst his guests as there had been before they had descended to the vault, also, he noted, not quite the same level of deference. The men had loosened their ties and were both smoking without so much as a 'by your leave'. The women sat fiddling, one with a button the other with her hat. At that moment Mihriban entered and apologised for being late. She took her seat and sat with the small velvet bag on her lap. The *directeur* raised his head smiled and looked round the room as though he was doing a head count, he then began to speak.

"My valued clients, I would like to bring the proceedings to a conclusion if you have no further requests? In the instructions we received from the late Valide Sultan, there was no provision as to how the inheritance was to be divided and this brings me to a point of some sensitivity. When the Ottoman Bank was founded there was within its articles a clause that waived all bank charges for services rendered to the royal family or the palace. However, when the Turkish Republic superseded the Ottoman Empire in 1923, new articles were drawn up to allow the bank to carry on its business and that clause was, obviously, not included. Let met get straight to the point, there have accrued certain bank charges, namely the safe keeping of the late Valide Sultan's strongbox. Before the bank can allow the afore mentioned to leave this property the outstanding bank charges must first be settled." The *directeur* looked at the faces to see if there was any reaction, they all sat stony faced. "Therefore calculating these charges as of 1923, with interest and taxes included, they come to a total of ..." He looked down and shuffled with the papers, coughed and then continued in a low voice. "One hundred and fifteen thousand Francs."

This created quite an indignant stir amongst the *directeur*'s guests. The man with the bushy moustache jumped to his feet, brushed the cigarette ash from his lapel and blurted out:

"*Monsieur le Directeur*, with the greatest respect, I wish to formally renounce any claim, present or future, to the inheritance so far referred to!" So saying, he turned and stormed out of the door.

The others rose to their feet muttering that they were in accord with their cousin and wishing the *directeur* 'good day' they hastily beat their retreat. The *directeur* stood, mouth open, looking towards the door, it was only then that he noticed that Mihriban remained still seated. Before he could say anything she spoke.

"*Monsieur le Directeur*, the hopes of an inheritance of substance from our great grandmother consist only of this small bag containing a few valueless papers. Therefore I hope you won't interpret the disappointment of my cousins as rudeness, as you probably have no idea of the financial hardship that this family has gone through. So saying, I would dearly like to keep this bag of papers as sign of respect and in accordance with the wishes of my late great grand-mother, however my financial circumstances are no different than those of my cousins. There is only one thing I can offer you to cover the cost of the bank charges and that is this diamond broach I am wearing here. It is a family heirloom and was a gift from my late mother."

The young woman removed the broach from her jacket and placed it on the desk in front of her and pushed it hesitantly towards the *directeur.* M. Chapus turned to M. Batchelet and after a whispered conversation turned back to Mihriban.

"Madam, our bank will be delighted to accept your broach in lieu of payment and in memory of her late majesty's wishes..."

Mihriban rose from her seat even though the *directeur* seemed determined to keep speaking and, in a demonstration of *noblesse oblige,* she gave an almost imperceptible curtsy, said 'good day, gentlemen' and turned leaving the room with her head held high much to the consternation of the two men scrambling to their feet.

That evening in her minute studio flat off the boulevard Saint Germain, she opened a an exceptional bottle of Medoc, one that she had been saving for a special occasion. She half filled her crystal glass, removed her great grand-mother's letter from the velvet bag and sat down by the window to complete reading it.

> Today is the twenty third day of the third month 1261, Hijre calendar (23rd March 1882). I am at the twilight of my life and I have therefore decided to write down an account that will be both a reflection of my emotions as well as the story of my life.
>
> I was never able to learn exactly when I was born. When I asked my mother she would reply that it was round about the time that Alemdar Pasha was killed. My childhood passed in abject poverty in the gypsy quarter of Sulukale beneath the old city walls. My father worked a horse drawn cart. Every morning he would get up and leave the house when it was still dark and he wouldn't return until it was night. What exactly he did I never did find out but I imagine that he collected scrap or rags and bones. My mother would get up even before him, she would prepare his so-called breakfast which was usually two or three stale slices of bread left over from the day before accompanied by a raw onion or a few olives. I never learnt what she did until I reached the age of seven and then she started to take me to work with her.

My mother was a washerwoman and bath attendant at the Çemberlitaş Hamamı. And at that tender age I was set to work with her. In the beginning I just did cleaning jobs but soon I was soaping the scrubbing cloths and massaging the bodies of the fat woman who came to the baths, I did this by walking on their backs while they lay on the Göbektası or hot stone. My mother always said my small feet were ideal for this work. After the customers had dressed my mother and I would stand by the door, bowed with careworn looks on our faces and our right hands extended. 'Health to you esteemed lady and God save the sultan!' We would say in order to try and squeeze out a halfpenny tip. But generally the customers brushed us aside and ignored us. But there were a few wealthy ladies who, while adjusting their veils before going out into the street, would deposit the halfpenny into my mother's hand without deigning to look at our faces.

While I was only ten years old my mother died. The boiler stoker, 'gnarled' Recep, killed her one day by striking her on the head with the shovel he used for the boiler. We put my mother's body onto my father's cart. It must have been a sight, my mother's body wrapped in old towels from the Hamam and my father's ancient cart pulled by his even older horse called 'Külhanbey' which had an unfortunate reference to stokers so from that day forth he was named 'Hayırsız' or 'Good for Nothing' instead. We took my mother to the pauper's cemetery at Kasimpasha. All through the journey my father kept repeating, 'Now I know why the bitch never brought any money home, she was giving it to that evil bastard!'

Six months after burying my mother, my father died. He was stabbed to death by a pederast gypsy called 'Tıyız Hamdi'. He had stabbed my father in the back when they couldn't come to an agreement on how they were going to divide up a pile of scrap they had collected together. I found his dead body at home when I returned from the Hamam. The neighbours said they had been alerted when his horse and cart had returned without him!

From that day on I started living in the baths. The owner had felt sorry for me because I was an orphan. After the last customer had gone and I had left the baths spick and span he allowed me to curl up in one of the changing stalls. I worked as hard as I could at being a good bathhouse attendant. Everyday I would scrub and pound the women and I would prepare the food they brought with them to eat by the pool in the cool room. When they started to dance and sing I would withdraw into a corner and watch them enjoy themselves. By observing carefully and playing the instrument when there was no one around I even learnt to play the lute. When the women heard how well I could play they would make sure that I played for them too. I soon became an indispensable part of the Çemberlitaş Hamamı and I started to collect a good wage in tips too. But it was all to no avail because the owner of the Hamam, 'Kara Tellak', would take from me every last penny I earned in tips. He was a frightening man, as big as the trunk of a black pine, dark and hairy. He claimed to have descent from a well-known family. I overheard the customers gossiping that when he let out a shout in Atikali it could be heard over a mile away at the Hippodrome! He would pay me only a farthing a day and I would use all of that to buy myself a pie and a yoghurt drink when I slipped out for a few minutes after work.

One afternoon when I had finished up at the Hamam and, as was my habit, I went for a walk from Çemberlitaş to Sultanahmet square. That particular day I was so tired I could hardly see where I was walking. Before I could understand what was happening, all about me were scattering like so many frightened chickens, I looked up to find myself in the path of a troop of cavalry bearing down on me at full gallop. The captain of the troop was slashing his crop frantically and shouting.

'Clear the way! Make way for the sultan!'

I couldn't move, I remained rooted to the spot and when the horse in front of me shied up I covered my eyes thinking it must be the end of me and when I felt its flank slam into my shoulders I was thrown to the ground unconscious. When I came to my senses I saw that I had been lain on the pavement by the side of the road. There was a pungent odour coming from the handkerchief that an officer, kneeling beside me, was holding to my nose. My over-garment was ripped and my hair had become unravelled. I felt another pair of eyes staring at me and when I turned my head, that was when I saw him for the first time. He was looking at me from the royal carriage with a look of deep concern on his face. The officer who had given me the smelling salts then put his hands under my arms to lift me to my feet. When he saw that I could stand unaided he ran over to the carriage. He saluted briskly and then said something to the sultan. The carriage and the cavalry then started to move off. As the carriage passed in front of me there was a moment when our eyes met again. I knew from that day on I would never remove those beautiful dark olive coloured eyes from my mind but I was still too young to understand why.

The following day, it must have been about midday, I heard a loud commotion in front of the bathhouse. At the time I was scrubbing the back of a noble woman called Rahime from the house of Oduncuzadeler. The head attendant came and pulled my arm. She told me to go and get dressed, gather my things and go to the front entrance immediately. I began to sob. I didn't want to be thrown out onto the street. The only thing I ever did wrong was to conceal ten copper coins that I had received as tips, surely they would overlook that as a childish error? After all I had been a good worker and had only ever asked for my food and board? By then I was sobbing uncontrollably. The head attendant pulled me to my feet. As she was trying to shake some reason in to me, she turned her eyes up to the heavens which, in this case, were the shafts of light coming from the dome of the Hamam.

'Oh holy God,' she said. 'You who hold the fate of us all; in an instant you can turn the rich and mighty into the weak and impoverished, or elevate an orphaned gypsy girl like this to the very highest! Dear Lord, answer my prayers too!'

I still did not understand what she meant but I was still frightened enough of her anger and the back of her hand to keep quiet and get dressed quickly. Besides the clothes I stood up in, the only possessions I had were the ten coins, which I was glad to say the head attendant had overlooked and a small box wood comb, which a customer had given to me when one of the teeth was broken. When I came to the door and saw the man waiting for me I almost passed out again. He was a giant of a black man with an even larger head on top of which was perched a blood red tasselled fez. I learnt later from the two elderly hand maidens who sat with me in the carriage as I was taken to the palace, that this man, now sitting next to the driver, was the Harem's head eunuch and his name was Cafer.

I will not go into too much detail about my first night in the palace. Suffice to say I was carefully prepared and brought before my sultan. But what I saw revealed in the olive dark eyes of my master I will hold hidden in my heart until judgement day.

I will always remember with gratitude how her highness, Valide Nakşidil Sultan, the queen mother, patiently helped me to adapt to life in the Seraglio. I was taught the court protocol as well as court manners and etiquette. I was also taught to speak French which greatly helped me to rise in my master's favour. She would always say the poverty of my former life and my race were of no importance at all, as all our lives were as dry leaves blown here and there in the winds of fate. On one occasion I heard her add, to herself or to me I couldn't be sure, that those selfsame winds had blown her as a small girl who enjoyed collecting sea shells, from a faraway island via a Barbary slave market to this celebrated palace and then to becoming the queen mother herself.

Receiving my instruction directly from the Valide Sultan meant I came to spend more time with my master, my dear Mahmud. He would discuss matters of state with her and even include me in these discussions. Following the Alemdar event he became more determined than ever to rid himself of the Janissary threat. He could trust no one. He would make notes in a black leather bound notebook, but he would write in a code language which no one would understand. When the 'Hayriye' incident occurred, he confided in me, barely controlling his laughter, that he wrote his notes in the Creole tongue of Martinique that his mother had taught him.

After many months of secret preparation the moment had come for Sultan Mahmud to meet his destiny. On that hot fateful June morning, having asked us for our blessing, he departed for the Sultan Ahmet mosque. After making his devotions he remained in silent prayer for some considerable time. He then went to where the sacred banner of the Prophet was kept. First he kissed it and then touched it to his brow. He then hoisted the banner in the air and cried:

"Oh God! Oh Mohammad! Oh fortitude! Oh salvation!"

He then took up his position at the head of his troops.

The reckoning lasted for three full days. The Janissary barracks received bombardment after bombardment. Not even a stone was left standing, their bodies were torn limb from limb. So violent were the explosions that we saw bloody Janissary corpses suspended in the old oak trees of the palace gardens like some macabre blossom. The sea was covered in corpses almost as far as Leander's tower at Scutari. The poor went hungry as their main source of food was fish from the Bosphorus and they refused to eat fish that might have gorged on human flesh. For those long days and nights I waited alone in the palace, the sound of cannon and the screams of the wounded giving no respite. Then on the fourth morning my Nubian maid, Nihal, brought me the news that my lion-hearted sultan had returned and was waiting impatiently to see me. It was one of the rare occasions that her inscrutable face broke into a grin. In one decisive move the sultan had wiped from the pages of history the Janissary threat, a threat that had buried the palace in the silt of torpidity for centuries.

My Mahmud passionately believed in making the proud Ottoman an equal to the modern European states. Following the purging of the Janissaries, given the name Vaka-I-Hayriye, he set about his reforms.

The state began to lick its wounds but, unfortunately, the claws of the Russian bear were always on our backs. As for the British lion, who we thought would ring and chain the bear, they had their own agenda of protecting their prey from others for later consumption by themselves! Our empire in the Balkans was shrinking by the hour. And the new modernised army was yet to reach full strength and when rushed prematurely to the fronts proved an easy mouthful for the Russians. Changing the name of regiments to 'Asakiri Mansure-I Muhammediye'(The soldiers of Mohammad charging to victory) did little to stem the tide of defeat.

Despite the modernisation of the army the Greek uprising exasperated Mahmud particularly with the support they received from abroad. He was turning to the bottle for solace more and more and the wine was beginning to sap his ability to be decisive or make sound judgements. In an irrational frenzy of anger he had the Greek Patriarch, Gregorius, strung up from the Patriarchate gate. The Patriarch had, in fact been condemning the uprising and had been preaching that the rebels would burn in hell for rebelling against the state that succoured them. The Muslim populace were stirred up to acts of violence and vandalism. Churches were broken in to and others were destroyed, most were ransacked. The schools the Greeks had founded in Phanar and Kuruçeşme as well as a university under construction in Cydonia were all razed to the ground. All of this severely dented the positive opinion of the Ottoman state that had been developing in Europe that namely here, at last, was a sultan who would modernise the country.

Mahmud turned to the Khedive of Egypt for aid in suppressing the Greek rebellion. The Khedive sent an army with his fleet to Mora under the command of his son Ibrahim. The landed and started advancing into the hinterland. Mahmud sent an Army from the north to link up with the Egyptians. Despite the arch rivalry between them, France, England and Russia sent a combined fleet to the aid of the Greek rebels. This huge force destroyed the Egyptian and Ottoman fleet at Navarin on October 20th 1827. Mahmud once again let his anger rule his head and rather than negotiating a cease fire so that he could consolidate his forces, he ordered instead, the immediate closure to all foreign shipping of the Bosphorus and Dardanelles, in March 1828. As a result of this declaration, Russia declared war on the Ottoman Empire the following month. After a year of fighting and on so many fronts we were all but finished. The Russian cavalry was advancing along the North Aegean coast and in the East they had made major gains, capturing Erzurum and Kars and were preparing to enter Trabzon.

A treaty was scrambled together and signed in Edirne in 1829 that gave us a small amount of breathing space. But not for long, now are former allies were turning against us. The Khedive of Egypt, Mehmed Ali Pasha, demanded Egypt, the Lebanon and Syria as reparation for the fleet he had lost fighting on behalf of the sultan. Again Mahmud's lack of diplomacy and passion was his downfall. He immediately responded by declaring the Khedive a traitor. Ibrahim Pasha, the Khedive's son once again took to the battlefield, and quickly advanced through Lebanon and Syria and entered into the Anatolian motherland. At Konya, he routed the army we sent to halt his advance. Mahmud saw that nothing now lay between Ibrahim and Constantiniye and, in blind panic, he turned to his erstwhile enemy for help, Russia. The Russians sent three warships to the Bosphorus shortly followed by an army of thirty thousand men. When they disembarked they camped at the Hunkar landing, and then, when all their supplies were landed, they moved their camp to the Büyükdere meadows. Ibrahim Pasha's advance was checked. The British and the French also sent ships through the Dardanelles and into the Bosphorus to support the sultan. A treaty was brokered and Ibrahim Pasha withdrew his army. Mahmud was not prepared to allow this treason to go unpunished but his health was declining. Cirrhosis was destroying his liver. In April of 1839 he took a fatal decision of putting his army under the fanatical and ignorant command of Hafiz Pasha. The army set out to the South-East on a mission of retribution. Thousands untrained and ill-equipped sons of the empire died in the searing heat of the Nizip desert. The news of the loss reached us as my sultan lay on his death bed. We decided not to tell him the fate of his army. My master passed from this life on the second of June.

My Mahmud's body was not even cold before the vultures gathered over the palace to grab what they could. Although I was the sultan's favourite it was his other favourite Bezmialem's son Abdulmecit who would be sultan. My son Abdulaziz and I withdrew from active official life and observed the turmoil from the sidelines and with great sadness. While the Russians were still camped at Beykoz, Husrev Pasha, who was known to be in the pay of the Czar, appropriated the seal and office of the Grand Vizier by force. The vultures and hyenas were determined to rip the great house of Ottoman to shreds even before the infidel had an opportunity to do so. The most treacherous of them all was Ahmet Fethi Pasha who, in act treason that surpassed the basest of history's traitors, had, before the alarm could be raised, sailed the whole Ottoman fleet from the Golden Horn and surrendered it intact to Mehmed Ali!

The new sultan followed his mother's advice and avoided any conflicts with Husrev Pasha. He sent to London, a well-educated and brilliant young man called Mustafa Resid, ostensibly to seek support from the British. Upon his return, to everyone's astonishment, he read a declaration to all the assembled foreign heads of mission. It became known as the '*Gülhane* Imperial Declaration' and was, in all intents and purposes, the beginning of the reform movement. A French ambassador would later confide in me that Resid's text was no more than a description of the British constitutional monarchy, and it was, more than likely, formulated for him when he was in London. None of this should take away from Bezmialem Sultan and her son's achievement and it gave us great contentment that he was determined to follow in the footsteps of my Mahmud. Soon after this, the five strongest European nations made a joint declaration, demanding that Mehmed Ali withdraw completely from Ottoman territory. Mehmed Ali was counting on French support and refused to comply. The British navy then bombarded the coastal towns of the Lebanon and Syria. This proved decisive and the Egyptian forces then withdrew from all the Ottoman territories including Crete.

However, there was no respite from the claws of our northern neighbour. During an audience with the sultan, the British ambassador to the Sublime Porte, Stratford Canning, relayed that the British Ambassador in St Petersburg, Sir Hamilton Seymour had been summoned by Tsar Nicolas to the court where he was told that if Britain intended an alliance with the Sublime Porte he should convey to his government that it was something that was totally unacceptable as access to the warm seas was Russia's historic right. He finished by saying that if Britain thought they could prolong the life of the 'Sick Man of Europe' they were dangerously mistaken. The Ambassador also added that they had information that the Russians were preparing for a war with the sole purpose of wresting as much territory as they could from the Ottoman Empire. The Ambassador concluded by saying that if this was truly the case Britain would not stand by as a spectator and requested that the sultan mobilise his forces accordingly.

The Tsar started to apply more pressure by appointing Prince Menchikof as his Ambassador to the Sublime Porte. The prince was a career soldier notorious for his cruelty in the field. He was completely blatant about why he was in Constantiniye, he said he wished to cause as much strife and division as possible in the state through corruption and coercion so that, when it came to war, the work of the Russian army would be that much easier! Stratford Canning was called back to London where he was honoured with a peerage becoming Lord Stratford de Redcliffe, and then sent straight back to Constantiniye, much to the anger of the Russians. War now appeared inevitable. The British diplomatic policy prior to the emergence of Mehmed Ali Pasha had been to play off the Russians against the French, now they reversed those roles and convinced the French that they should join forces in the noble cause of opposing the Russian threat! For the British, 'commerce' was always a noble cause.

The Crimean War did not last for long. The key to the war was the Port of Sevastopol, which eventually fell to the allies after the British navy blockaded and then bombarded the port. Despite the British desire to prolong the war and truly draw the nails of the Russian Bear, the French had already entered into secret negotiations that ended with the Treaty of Paris. The treaty stipulated that Russia would withdraw from all Ottoman territory and that the Sublime Porte would abide by the articles of reform that had been drafted in the *'Gulhane Declaration'*, namely that there should be equality for all subjects of the empire and that no foreign forces would be tolerated interfering in the internal affairs of the state. I heard later from a good source that Canning said to a colleague that, as war reparation, he was hoping for a declaration of total sovereignty for Constantiniye and that he wished his hands had broken so that he would not have to have signed that 'ignoble paragraph'.

In the wake of the Paris Treaty the European powers opened up their coffers to us, or so it appeared. The first loans were for the purpose of covering our Crimean war expenses but then further requests followed from Sultan Abdulmecit. However, when the collateral and brokers fees were deducted barely half of the negotiated millions of pounds in loans actually ever reached the treasury. Sultan Abdulmecit had given a blank cheque to the Armenian Architect Balyan to build him a palace on the *Dolmabahçe* shore of the Bosphorus that would surpass that of any of the European royal houses. He was also on good terms with my son Abdulaziz for whom he was building two equally imposing Bosphorus palaces, the *Çırağan* and Beylerbeyi palaces as well as restoring the Sadabat mansion. As Abdulmecid spent the money from these loans like water he was cut down by tuberculosis and died at the end of June 1861. Thus began the most auspicious period of my whole adventure filled life. My lion of a son Abdulaziz ascended to the throne and I became the Queen Mother.

After my son's inauguration I got it into my head that it was now the time to visit the fabled cities of Europe that my mentor, Murad's mother Nakşidil Sultan, had told me all about. I am not sure how, but I convinced my son, despite the strong objections of Midhat and Ziya Pashas, that it would be a fine venture. And so we set out, the first time in the history of the great Ottoman Empire that a sultan visited the great cities of Europe: Naples, Paris, London, Berlin and Budapest. I, your great grandmother, the one time bathhouse attendant Besime, was now visiting and being feted in the lands that my dear Sultan Mahmud could only read about in books or visit in his dreams. Noble kings and Archdukes raised my hand to their lips, queens showered me with compliments, great statesmen bowed their heads before me. What do you think of that Kara Tellak! If you had known that this would be the fate of the little gypsy girl you kept locked in your bathhouse you would have become rooted to the spot!

After returning from our European tour I felt there was nothing left that I craved for in this life. As the queen mother Nakşidil Sultan often told me, the winds of fate had blown me from the cinders of the bathhouse furnace to the cool towers of an ivory castle. I was fully aware that anything accumulated in this world stays right here when our time comes to leave this mortal coil. So I started to dedicate my life to good works. I knew better than anybody about the abyss of poverty and could understand the suffering of the poor like no one else. I started to use money from the treasury to help the poor and destitute, the unfortunate and homeless in every little way that I could. I also decided that I had to demonstrate my thankfulness to the Almighty for all the mercies he had bestowed upon me. To that end I decided to have a mosque built in my name similar to the one Bezmialem Sultan had built next to the new palace at Dolmabahçe. Although there had always been a sense of rivalry about our respective sons' rights to the succession, we had at all times been on friendly terms. However, I wanted more than just a place of worship, I wanted there to be a school and a soup kitchen attached to the building for the benefit of the poor as well as other annexes. I gave instructions to the architects to commence work right away.

Meanwhile, the tap that had allowed the flood of funds to flow was being turned off. Money had been in abundance even for the Abdulaziz's cock fight and ram fight extravaganzas. My son had over one thousand concubines and many of the favourites were spending money like water. They even ordered clothes and jewellery to be shipped from Europe. Ziya Pasha constantly warned of the drain on treasury finances so much so that my son wanted rid of him. On one occasion I asked Ziya if he was really our enemy. He replied that the real enemies of the state appeared to be us and he showed me just one page from the account books he had brought with him. I was astonished to see that one of my son's favourites, a Circassian beauty called Mihri, had had more than a million Sterling Pounds channelled to her in the course of that year. Almost all the pashas in the state administration were either corrupt or taking bribes. They all, without exception, possessed mansions, concubines and fortunes in gold bullion. Even the Grand Vizier Mahmud Sevket was receiving bribes from the Russian Ambassador, Ignatiev. The foreign banks were now continuously hammering on the door. We received a constant stream of letters and demands from the foreign ambassadors on behalf of their banks and financial institutions in their respective countries. It was a black day on October 6, 1875 when we were forced by our foreign creditors to declare the state bankrupt while the whole world watched on. From then on the finances of the state in the discharging of debts was to be in the hands of the Office of Public Debt located in a stone building dominating the Galata heights, I am told the building resembled the old Bastille prison.

The assassination of the French and Greek consuls in Thessalonica was the beginning of the end for us. The foreign powers were outraged and were making unveiled threats of military retaliation. Within the country the leaders of the 'Young Turk' movement we fermenting open revolt. One Friday thousands of people gathered round the palace waiting for the royal carriage taking Abdulaziz to Friday prayers. I persuaded my son that it wouldn't be prudent to leave the palace. Sadly, it became the first occasion in the long glorious history of the House of Ottoman that a sultan failed to attend Friday prayers. The following day the leaders of the Young Turks came to the palace with their list of demands. The most pressing of these was the immediate replacement of the Grand Vizier. My son was close to a nervous breakdown so I went to confront them in his place. The ministers and officials of state would have hid under their chairs if they could, they were quaking with fear as to what fate lay in store for them at the hands of the Young Turks. For me they represented no threat so that I harangued them instead. They were completely taken aback, and making their excuses bowed and said they would return later.

On the 29th May, 1876, we woke up to find the palace grounds deserted, we soon realised that the Young Turks had manage to persuade the palace guard commander and his men to join their side. We then received rumours that my son's nephew, Murad, was being brought from Prinkipo in the Princes' Islands to be placed on the throne in place of my son. Nothing happened all day and when we retired we knew we still had loyal guards within the palace. But around midnight Rusdi Pasha, persuaded the last remaining loyal guards not to put up any resistance and he had entered the palace with his treacherous henchmen. By the aid of only moonlight they had passed through the throne room and entered our private quarters. When confronted by the head of the Harem, Cafer, they just brushed him aside. But while they were trying to light a candelabra they managed to drop it to the floor. The noise woke up my son who flew out of his chamber in the direction from where the noise had come. Just as he was about to lay his hands on the traitor Rusdi, the Circassian girl with whom he had spent the night came running from the chamber and threw herself at his feet and wrapping herself around his legs pleaded with him to calm down and not to do anything that would cause him hurt. Her pleas fell on deaf ears but as he was trying to free himself from her hysterical grasp I burst in with even more anger that my son was displaying. I was livid, how dare they not only invade the palace but enter the sacred Harem too? I grabbed the first thing I could lay my hands on. A weighty candelabra that I swung at the first person within distance, cracking him around the head. Rusdi shouted out that I should stay my hand and do no more damage as our cause was already lost. He told me that the palace was surrounded and that we were not to be harmed but only exiled to the old Seraglio where we would pass the rest of our days. He stepped forward and gently removed the candelabra from my hand. I knew it was all over and turned to my son who was still trying to un-entangle himself from the hysterical girl. I told him to give up the struggle and that we had to accept out fate. My words hit my son like lighting does a proud tree. His huge, hundred and thirty kilo wrestlers frame, crumbled like a split trunk. He turned to me with all vitality drained from his eyes and asked me if it could be true that we were to be no more. I did not want him to weep in front of those traitors so I took his arm and led him into my chamber. At the door I turned to Rusdi and asked him to give us until morning so that we could collect ourselves. But it was only a few hours later when we were taken by caique from the Dolmabahçe landing across the

Bosphorus to the Topkapı Seraglio which had been the seat of my son's dynasty for so many centuries and that now, bathed in moonlight, was to be our final home.

Howeve,r things didn't turn out as we expected and it wasn't to be a long sojourn after all. A day later we were taken to the Çırağan palace. My first instinct was that this was a good omen, but I was to be proved bitterly wrong. Three days later our faithful servant Cafer, knelt down before me and with tears welling up in his eyes told me that the sultan had taken his own life. In all honesty, he had been showing signs of eccentricity but when they said he had slashed his wrists with a pair of scissors, I could do nothing but pretend to agree with this pack of lies. In private, I prayed for God to bring down his wrath on those who perpetrated this crime. That wrath did not take long to manifest itself. Only a few days passed before another tragedy, Mihri, the favourite of my son's who was notorious for her extravagance, died in childbirth. A loyal maid still working at the palace relayed to me what happened. Mihri's corpse was put in a simple coffin decorated with her cashmere shawl and covered in roses. A procession of people followed the coffin to the cemetery, many of them weeping aloud at this tragic loss. What then befell the new owners of the palace convinced me that it must be cursed. Mihri's brother, Hasan, left the procession half way to the cemetery and returned to the palace. This mighty Circassian forced his way into the council chamber as the council of ministers was in session. He drew out a gun and killed the first person he encountered, Huseyin Avni, with a single shot. He then grabbed a sword and made as if to remove the victim's head. Midhat Pasha and the others then tried to overpower him. They say that Rasid Pasha was rooted to the spot dumbstruck with fear. The Admiralty minister, Ahmed Pasha, jumped on to Hasan's back, but the mighty Circassian threw him off as if he was of no more significance than a flea. Hasan had descended like the Grim Reaper on those base usurpers who had seized the throne from us. He then turned his anger on Rasid who was still anchored to the spot. The others grabbed this opportunity to flee the chamber and into a side room where they locked the heavy mahogany doors behind them. Hasan threw his full weight against the door bellowing out that he would not hurt anyone in there as long as they surrendered the Admiralty minister. The heavy doors looked as though they would give way and the petrified cowards inside put their shoulders to the door while pleading with Hasan to consider carefully what he was doing. This enraged Hasan still further and he fired twice at the door, drilling the Grand Vizier on the other side. Midhat Pasha had found a side door to the room and had taken advantage of this by circling round behind Hasan and bringing his men with him. Hasan shot two of them but could only wound Midhat. Then he killed an officer and wounded seven others in the next wave of attackers causing an English journalist, who just happened to be there, to soil his pants. But by now Hasan was finally overpowered. The maid who relayed this to me had been a witness to this whole wonderful act of revenge. She then learnt from one of the soldiers guarding him about what happened next. Hasan was chained and thrown into a cell ready to be hung the following day. He showed no sign of remorse or regret and spent a great part of the night in laughter and the rest in song. He sang the same song over and over again so that when the soldier came to tell the maid of what had happened the next day he could even still sing the melody and she, being a bright young thing, could repeat it to me as she retold the story. I recognised the melody instantly. It was an aria that my son and I had heard when we visited Naples. They had staged a great show in our honour. It was the first and only time we attended what we learnt to call the Opera. It was this particular aria that had most impressed my son. So much so that he went out of his way not to just learn its name, it was called 'Lucia di Lammermoor', but to learn to sing it too. When we returned to the palace he would perform it to his favourite Mihri just to see the look of astonishment on her face. She must have memorised it too and taught it to her brother. Immediately following morning prayers, they hung the mighty Circassian from a mulberry tree in the garden of a tea house facing Serasker Square.

After the death of my son, I turned the attention of my twilight years to helping the poor, the instruction of young children and prayer. After all, we owe our very existence to Allah, it is given and taken as the Creator chooses. I spent more and more of my time in the mosque I had constructed. But as my life runs its final course, I felt like looking forward to a new millennium and sharing some of what I have lived with my great grandchildren of the future. I therefore withdrew to my quarters and wrote this testament. And the bequest I leave of ten small copper coins and a damaged boxwood comb can only be the bequest of bathhouse attendant Besame, can it not? It couldn't possibly be that of the Valide Sultan, could it? But surely for the one who reads this testament and who doesn't begrudge giving a prayer in my memory these ten copper coins could become one hundred, or five hundred, or even a thousand. Half of what there is could provide instruction to the poor in my name and the remainder would give an opportunity for a life in pursuit of knowledge and adventure, similar to that of their great grandmother's.

Whoever reads and understands will be the beneficiary of my plea.

Signed: "Mehd-i Ulya-yi Saltanat Ismetli
Pertevniyal Valide Sultan"
(*The Tuğra*[22] seal of Sultan Abdulaziz)

Mihriban remained curled up and motionless in the armchair in which she had settled to read the letter. Eventually she sat up and filled her glass with what remained of the Medoc. She started to smile and then raised her glass in a toast.

"To you, my glorious gypsy great grandmother, may your soul rest in peace and rise in glory!"

She wanted to get up but the excitement of her great grandmother's testament could now no longer compete with the soporific effect of the wine and she now felt that perhaps a nap was what was called for.

When the telephone rang she really did not want to stir, after all she had only just closed her eyes, but when she did force an eye open she was taken aback to see the morning sunshine streaming into the room. She stretched out an arm and fumbled for the phone.

"Bonjour Madam, I am André Chapus of the Ottoman Bank."

"Excuse me, who did you say?"

"André Chapus? You were in my office yesterday?"

"Oh yes, I am sorry. What can I do for you Monsieur Chapus?"

'not much, I hope' Was what Mihriban was thinking to herself. She was already smarting from the loss of the family heirloom, the diamond broach, she hoped against hope that there wasn't some other expense he had overlooked.

"Madam, there is an important question I wish to ask of you."

"Please go ahead M. Capus."

"Have you had time to read the testament of your great grandmother, the Queen Mother?"

"Why yes, yes I have. But what possible significance could that have?"

"What significance? Well, as you recall, yesterday in my office, the other noble beneficiaries gave up any claims they might have

22. Tuğra: Sultan's seal.

to the late Queen Mother's estate. Only you wished to pursue that claim and offered in return your broach to cover the bank expenses. It was a gesture that truly impressed us. You are, without doubt, a true noble in the best sense of the word."

Mihriban took the receiver from her ear and looked at it for a second, 'what on earth can this man want at this time in the morning' she thought to herself. 'I wouldn't be surprised if he even asked for a date next'

"Are you still there Madam?"

" Yes, M. Chapus, but I must confess that I have a very busy day. Please don't consider me rude, but if I were to ask you to come to the point?"

"I'm sorry. Of course, of course. The problem is this, there is still one outstanding account that, because it has the prefix 'CI', is clearly one that belongs to the royal family. 'CI' stands for *'Compte Impérial'*. We obviously wish to liquidate this account too and give it to its rightful owner. The only problem is that this is a coded account and can only be accessed if the correct account code is given. Now, you will understand that I am getting to the point of my call. My suspicion is that this account was opened by your great grandmother and I wondered if you had found any reference to it or the account code when you were reading her testament?"

Mihriban, did not answer. She was trying to grasp the true dimensions of what this could mean while at the same time thinking back to the testament and what her great grandmother had written.

"You see madam," M. Chapus continued. "There is some urgency in this matter. If this account is not claimed in the next two days it will be appropriated by the French state. There is also more than a little sensitivity to this because this is not the channel I should be using to locate the beneficiary of this account...of course, if you should be able to locate the account code there will be a very small commission to pay but nothing like the expenses incurred on the safebox."

Mihriban thanked M. Chapus for his candidness and said that she would look at the testament again and call him back should she discover anything. She put the phone down and started to look at the sheets of paper that made up her great grandmother's testament. She picked up the final page and read this sentence aloud in the hope it would give her inspiration: *'But surely for the one who reads this testament and who doesn't begrudge giving a prayer in my memory these ten copper coins could become one hundred, or five hundred, or even a thousand'*

"Oh dear, dear, great grandmother, if you could only give some kind of clue!" Mihriban let out a sigh and lifted the velvet bag that had held the papers and emptied it out catching two of the copper coins in the palm of her hand. "Now tell me, just how can ten copper coins become one hundred?" But as the words left her mouth an idea struck her like a sharpened dart. She collected pen and paper and sat down on the edge of the dining table and wrote. '10-100-500-1000'. Could it really be as simple as that? Why not? Wasn't this what all bank accounts looked like? She picked up the phone and called M. Chapus. Trying hard to conceal her excitement she told him she might have found something. They agreed to meet at his office an hour later.

After entering Rue Meyerbeer Mihriban told the taxi driver to stop in front of the bank building. She was not kept waiting and was, within minutes, sitting once again on the other side of the *directeur's* expansive desk.

"I think I have found what we are looking for monsieur *le directeur.*"

"I can't express how happy that would make me!"

"And I imagine you will be also quite relieved if I can close this account."

"To its rightful owner? Of course. Now if you can show me the coded account number you have, we must check its authenticity first as the account can only be liquidated in the presence of the board of the bank and the government financial officer."

Mihriban hesitated wondering if her excitement might have been a little premature. She took a deep breath and pushed the piece of paper on which she had written the numbers across the desk towards M. Chapus. His expression changed even before he picked it up.

"I am afraid this not complete. There needs to be a six letter sequence, there," He stretched out a finger and pointed at the space, "Before the numbered sequence. You didn't come across anything like that by chance?"

Mihriban's optimism drained from her as did the blood from her face.

"No, no, when I discovered this sequence I was convinced that it was all that was required and looked no further."

"Well, there is still a little time. If you were to go back and look again?"

Mihriban did not answer at first but stared at the Utrillo original hanging on the *directeur's* wall. 'Dear great grandmother, you have revealed so much, don't leave me now! Even with my expensive private education my intelligence pales beside your untutored genius!' Just as her great grandmother had spoken to her so intimately over the centuries, Mihriban now appealed to her in her imagination. 'Or perhaps I should be addressing you as you signed your testament, *Mehd-i Ulya-yi Saltanat Ismetli Pertevniyal Valide Sultan...*' Mihriban rose to her feet lent across the desk, snatched a pen from a pen holder and pulling the piece of paper she had written the numbers on added a prefix of MUSIPVS and pushed the paper back across the desk to towards the *directeur.*

"Could this be it?"

"Let me see, yes, yes, that is more like it but don't forget that it must be a six letter sequence, you have written seven here."

Once again Mihriban felt the rug pulled out from under her. Just as she slumped back in her chair she heard M. Chapus snap his fingers and mutter a mild expletive under his breath.

"I do apologise. You are absolutely right! Imperial accounts always had seven letter prefixes! If you would be so kind as to wait in my office it shouldn't take more than an hour to arrange an extraordinary board meeting and summon the ministry representative." He exclaimed, getting to his feet excitedly; but he paused before he rushed from the room and, giving a short formal bow, said. "Madam, I congratulate you from the bottom of my heart."

In no more than fifty minutes the extraordinary board meeting had been convened. Together with the board members, Mihriban and the government finance officer had taken their places at the board room table. The government finance officer rose to his feet and addressed Mihriban.

"Ma'am, would you be so kind as to repeat the coded account number you provided for M. Chapus to those of us assembled here."

Mihriban felt the weight of history on her as she removed the piece of paper from her bag. She was doing this for great grandmother as much as she was doing it for herself. She took a deep breath and read out the sequence of letters and numbers she had so carefully and with so much expectation written on the paper. He wrote each one down as she dictated them and then he repeated them to the room.

"MUSIPVS 10-100-500-1000. I whole heartedly congratulate you ma'am on your excellent good fortune!"

The whole table beamed at her while M. Chapus led the applause. Mihriban was lost for words and then she remembered her great grandmother and spoke two words with Besime's once famous candidness:

"How much?"

"Her majesty the Queen Mother, opened the account on 5th October 1876, exactly twenty four hours before the Ottoman state filed for bankruptcy, she deposited one million Pounds Sterling in gold Sovereigns."

Mihriban's head started to spin and the shock of it began to make her feel a touch nauseous. The government representative was still talking.

"...with compound interest applied to it for a term of 120 years the account is now currently worth thirty seven million two hundred and twenty one thousand sixty three Pounds and ten pence. After tax and various deductions the net amount is approximately twenty eight million Pounds."

The Air France Concorde waited punctually on the apron of Charles de Gaulle airport. The pilot announced that ten minutes after take off they would reach supersonic speed and the flying time to Rio Janeiro would be three hours and fifty minutes. Mihriban was flying first-class and filling the time before take-off by working on a biography of her great grandmother on her laptop. She was sure that as soon as it was published the generous advance she had received would be fully justified as the story was as compelling as it was true. From the side table she took her glass of Dom Perignon and raised it to her lips. She chose one of the small canapés, generously piled with Beluga caviar, and popped it in her mouth without taking her eyes from the screen. The announcement to switch off electronic equipment was still to be made and she was connected to the internet with her mobile phone. Almost instantly the 'You Have Got Mail' window came up on her screen. She opened the waiting message:

Dear Mihriban,

It gives me the greatest pleasure to inform you that the Besime University has been officially opened today in a ceremony attended by the President of Turkey.

You will be receiving the audited accounts shortly but the total cost from ground-breaking until this moment has been a little short of ten million Pounds Stirling. In accordance with your instructions a fund of four million Pounds Sterling has been created to pay the fees and expenses of needy students. After the president cut the ribbon he referred in his speech to the immense generosity of the anonymous benefactor who had made the foundation of this university possible. He also referred to the benefactor's mission to provide higher education for young people who might not normally be able to afford it while, at the same time, providing all with an education that draws on the patrimony of the past by carrying it forward into the future.

You will amongst other things be receiving regular reports on the progress and success of your foundation.

Yours sincerely

Mihriban was interrupted by the friendly face of the flight attendant.

"Excuse me madam, but if I could ask you to turn off your electronic equipment we are now about to take off. You can turn on your lap-top again when the seat belt sign is switched off, but I am afraid you can't use your mobile phone until we have landed in Rio. Would you like some more champagne before we take off?"

The Doubled Headed Eagle's Last Flight

The corridors of the White House were full of their usual frenetic activity. President Wilson sat in the his private quarters trying to summon up the same level of energy in himself after a leisurely fishing trip to Annapolis. He was on his third cup of Colombian Mocha when he pressed the bell on his desk to summon his private secretary James Dunley. The secretary knocked on the door and entered carrying the President's black leather bound appointments diary in his hand.

"Good morning Mr. President."

"Listen Jim, I have decided that it might be more fitting to receive my guest in the gazebo in the rose garden rather than in the Oval Office. It is a beautiful day for the time of year and what's more it would be good to escape the confinements of the office. Please have the garden furniture placed there and can you arrange that we are provided with coffee, toasted bread and fresh orange juice."

"A very good decision if I might say so, Mr. President. When Ambassador Morgethau arrives I will escort him there myself. Do you wish me to be present to take notes?"

"I don't think that will be necessary. All you have to record is that the President had a private meeting with an old acquaintance on this day..."

"The 5th November 1923, sir."

"Exactly. That will be all, Jim."

"Very good, Mr. President. The gazebo will be ready in fifteen minutes. When your guest comes I will conduct him there and then inform you of his arrival."

The gazebo was on the southern end of the rose garden. The

president and his guest sat opposite each other in rattan chairs deep in conversation. A conversation that was punctuated with the occasional smile and flash of humour as only two old friends comfortable with each other can produce. President Wilson downed the glass of orange juice and brought it down sharply on the table interrupting the US ambassador to Constantinople.

"I couldn't agree with you more! It doesn't matter if it is Byzantine Constantinopolis or Turkish Istanbul, its position has, and always will be, pivotal. The great powers have always had their eyes on it. And, as you say, despite the deprivations of history, its natural beauty still justify its title as the 'Queen of Cities'"

"You know, there was something Napoleon said to his generals after he had put the 'lights out' all across Europe: 'Gentlemen, still the essential question remains, who will be master of Constantinople?'"

"After the turmoil of the last nine years the fact that the Turks have regained control of Istanbul denotes a new chapter in history. I have always been a champion of nations determining their own destiny, but I would like to hear from your own mouth an account of these events that have shaped a new world order. After all, you have followed it all from its epicentre in Istanbul."

Ambassador Morgenthau picked up a thick file he had brought with him and removed two photographs from it. The first of these he placed on the table in front of the president. The picture showed a striking uniformed man with the black lamb's skin *kalpak* on his head. Even in the photograph you could see the glint of determination, courage and ambition in his eyes.

"Mr. President, as you well know, Mustafa Kemal. From the very outset he impressed with his military genius but no one imagined that he could be a statesman too and has, of course, gone on to become one of the real winners of this war."

The ambassador placed the second picture over the first. In this picture the military uniform was replaced by the civilian evening wear of the modern statesman. The Ambassador looked up at the president and continued his account.

"A few days ago in Ankara, Mustafa Kemal announced to the world the founding of a new state, the Republic of Turkey. He has managed to create something that those that drew up the map for the treaty of Sèvres could never have imagined."

The president picked up the two pictures as though he was

weighing them in his hands. He nodded at the ambassador before speaking.

"Indisputably my dear friend. At the very moment that the 'sick man of Europe' appeared to be giving his last breath a strong new Turkish Republic emerges that can proudly take its place amongst the community of nations. But I observe you start this story from the end, could you possibly go back to the beginning so I can see how this all falls in to place?"

"Well, when the first shot was fired that would lead to war, the Western missions in Istanbul watched events unfold with considerable trepidation. However, there was one certainty from this titans struggle amongst the European powers that was about to unfold, and that was that the strategic significance of the Bosphorus and the Dardanelles was to be of paramount importance. For nearly one hundred years the British had conducted their 'Great Game' diplomacy and by supporting the Sublime Porte had thwarted the expansionist ambitions of first the French and then the Russians. This balance was upset with the fallout from the Balkans War which was, in many ways a prelude to the Great War, when the reformist movement called the 'Young Turks' came to prominence. The leaders were three opportunist generals called Enver, Talat and Cemal Pashas who soon had their hands on the reins of power and controlled the empire. Enver Pasha, perhaps the most ambitious, was also related to the sultan and saw the Germans as the new emerging 'über' power of Europe and, with them as allies, he dreamed of uniting all the Turkic peoples from Europe through to East Asia in a Pan-Turanic empire with himself at the head. Talat was actually descended from Pomak Gypsies and a giant of a man. Of the three he was the one who was concerned with the day to day running of the state. Cemal was the junior of the three and carried out the orders of the other two. Between them they turned Istanbul into a German military camp.

Prior to the war the Ottoman Navy had been under the command of an English Admiral, Arthur Limpus. In order to strengthen and modernise the fleet he requested that the Sublime Porte procure two new battleships. Cemal Pasha was keen on the idea and proposed a donation campaign starting in the provinces of Anatolia, he calculated that with sufficient patriotic sacrifice from the Turkish people it would not take long to raise the required three and a half million Pounds. In this he was right and soon the battleships were being built in the Armstrong and Vickers shipyards. They were launched and given the names Resadiye and Sultan Osman. But while they were still being commissioned in British waters the first flames that would ignite the Great War were crackling in the Balkans. Alliances had not as yet been struck but it was clear to the Lord of the Admiralty, Winston Churchill, that Enver, Cemal and Talat's allegiances lay with Germany and he appropriated the two ships for the British Navy. This decision outraged the Turks, seeing as the ships had been bought by popular subscription, and whatever decision they might have been considering, this action settled the matter and triggered the chain of events that would change the dimensions of the war."

The ambassador pointed towards the coffee pot, the president gestured his acquiescence and then placed the same hand on his chin as he considered what his ambassador had so far related. Ambassador Morgenthau refreshed their coffees as the servants had been told not to disturb them. He sat down and continued where he left off.

"Immediately following the declaration of war between Britain and Germany it appeared at first that the outcome of the war would be settled at sea between their two navies. Most of the Embassies had moved to their summer residencies on the Bosphorus near Tarabya in order to retain a more discrete presence.

We learned from a diplomatic courier who had travelled on the merchant ship Sicily that the British were in pursuit of two German cruisers. The consensus of opinion was that the two cruisers were trying to make for the Dardanelles and from there to Istanbul. Like it or not the conflict was escalating.

On the 11th August 1914 I paid a visit on the German Ambassador at his Tarabya summer residence to sound him out about how he interpreted these events. When I was presented to Ambassador Wangenheim I could see immediately that he was very agitated. He could hardly control his excitement. He was flushed and sweating and could hardly sit still. He greeted me as always in a cordial manner, but he was for ever craning out of the window that overlooked the Bosphorus. We talked but he was hardly concentrating on what was said. I decided to make my excuses and visit him at an other, more convenient time. I got to my feet to excuse myself when he, now even more excitedly, jumped to his and insisted that I stay as it was to be an historic day for both Germany and the world and that he wanted me to know of it before anyone else did.

The Ambassador, still leaving me standing, bounded over to the communications room door where an officer was standing with a message transcript in his hand. He read the deciphered message and then throwing his hands in the air, danced a small jig in centre of the room letting out shouts of joy. He then turned to me waving the message. 'We have shown those bastards!' He shouted, looking at me for congratulation. I was still none the wiser and asked him which 'bastards' he was referring to? 'The English, of course!' He boomed, his face a picture of glee. He excitedly explained that HMS Gloucester had given up the chase of the Breslau and Goeben somewhere off the island of Bozcaada and that the two warships had now entered Turkish waters at the Dardanelles. He was pacing the room still waving the message like a victorious schoolboy. Seeing that I still hadn't grasped the significance of it all he became more serious and explained still waving the message in my face that the warships had, in fact been given to the Turks and that their commander, admiral Souchen, and their crews would come under the flag and command of the Sultan. Still exultant he went over to the window and continued to talk to me with his backed turned. He said that this time the Teutons would not make the same mistake the Charlemagne the Great had made a thousand years earlier when he declined to unite the empires of the West and East again by accepting the hand of the Byzantine Empress Irene. This time there would be no mistake they were going to take their Byzantine inheritance from the descendants of Mehmed the Conqueror!

Well as you know, two days later the German cruisers Breslau and Goeben arrived in Istanbul. The triumvirate at the head of the Young Turks wasted no time and had the star and crescent flown on the sterns of the ships. The names of the ships were changed to the Midilli and the Sultan Selim; the latter was later changed to the Yavuz the moniker of Suleyman the Magnificent's father Selim the Grim. The ships were anchored in *Büyükdere* bay opposite the Russian mission. The German crews changed their uniforms and donned the fez in place of their usual *Kaiserliche* Marine caps.

Mr. President, it was quite an impressive sight to see these German sailors standing on their decks singing the German national anthem and other patriotic songs, taunting the Russians in their fezzes with the star and crescent flying from their mast heads.

We received reports that the Turkish government had not all been in agreement with this de facto alignment with the Germans by the acceptance of these ships. Enver Pasha put an end to this opposition by removing his pistol from its holster and placing it on the table in front of him. The opposition begrudgingly gave their consent. The following day the ships had sailed north into the Black Sea and a day later were shelling Odessa with their Turkish colours flying proud for all to see. It only took a few days for Russia to declare that they were now at war with the Ottoman Empire.

There was a story circulating that the finance minister Cavit Bey chanced upon a Belgian diplomat of his acquaintance while out walking in the Banking district. He took the Belgian by the arm and led him aside. He looked around before telling him in an urgent whisper that he had very sad news to convey, and revealed that the Germans were on the point of seizing Brussels. The Belgian diplomat seemed completely undaunted by this news and turned to Cavit Bey and announced in a loud voice that he had even sadder news to convey and that was that the Germans had already taken Istanbul.

On the 27th September 1914, Enver and his cronies relieved Admiral Limpus of his command of the Ottoman Navy and the Dardanelles were closed to all Allied shipping.

Looking back in hindsight at these events it is clear to me that the British made a serious tactical error in confiscating the Turkish ships. Had they allowed them to be delivered crewed by an British crew it could have had a completely different impact on public opinion and thus Turkey's participation in the war. As it was, these ships had been paid for by public subscription, even children had saved and donated money and then there were their names, Resadiye and Osman, the latter being the revered founder of the Ottoman dynasty. Even the most anglophile of Turks lost their patience after this.

The war years are well documented, the allies heavy defeat at Gallipoli, the Russian Revolution and their declaration of neutrality and then the entry of the US into the war with the armistice that followed soon after. But I would like to relate an event which occurred while I was still in Istanbul. After the Bolsheviks had driven all before them about twenty thousand White Russian refugees, mostly aristocrats, land owners and army officers escaped to Istanbul. One day when I was walking in the Grande Rue de Pera, close to our mission I came face to face with a couple and despite the lady having her face concealed by the veil of her hat and the gentleman attempting the same by turning up the collar of his topcoat, I recognised them immediately. The man was the former pre-revolutionary Russian ambassador to the Sublime Porte. I almost had to coerce the former ambassador and his wife to join me for coffee in the Café Marquise. The reason became immediately clear, they were totally impoverished. He was now trying to eke out a living by giving private lessons. At first he was reticent to give any further details about their current circumstances but after I plied him with two glasses of vintage Cognac to accompany the coffee he became more talkative. I ordered more cognac and I overheard the blonde waitress as she placed the glass in front of him say something sarcastically to him in Russian that made him stiffen. When I pressed him as to what the waitress had said his eyes filled with tears. He raised his glass to his lips and downed it and one and then looking as though he would smash it on the floor but brought it down heavily on the table instead. His wife took his hand and said something to soothe him. It seemed to do the trick. He patted her hand and turned to me more calmly. He said that life was like an opiate, lulling you, as though in a dream, into a false sense of the eternal, only for it to remove everything you have leaving you floundering in your helplessness. He exemplified this by saying that our waitress had been the Countess Katuska. Her family had owned estates near St Petersburg as big as Belgium, they had had seven hundred thousand peasants working the land. She had said to him that when he was next invited by the Tsar to the Hermitage to say to his majesty that she was unable to be present because she had more pressing business to attend to!

There was no stopping the former ambassador now. He said that Russia was a mother that devoured her own children. He said that for nearly two hundred years that Britain had, through her influence and power, thwarted Russia's ambitions as heirs to the Byzantine Empire. Ever since Constantinople fell to the Turk, its name in Russia had been Tsargrad, or city of the Tsar. He said that Russians felt they were destined to be the third Roman empire with Tsargrad at its heart and that the Byzantium was theirs by right. I couldn't stop him now as he gave me the history of these ambitions. How Catherine the Great had instigated an 'Eastern Project' and how she had plans to place a puppet king in the city in place of the sultan. This is why she had her second son christened Constantine and had him instructed in the Greek language and its history. When she annexed the Crimea in 1784 she took her commander-in-chief Grigori Potemkin with her to meet with the Austro-Hungarian Emperor Joseph. The purpose of the meeting was to demonstrate her military successes and to ask for his alliance in a war against the Ottoman Empire. To this end she had the emperor pass under a triumphal arch embellished with golden laurel leaves bearing the legend 'To Byzantium'. The former ambassador said that they had come closest to realising their dream in the war of forty years before when they had advanced as far as the old Byzantine walls of the city, only to be turned back by the threat of a barrage from the British fleet anchored off shore in the sea of Marmara. He said that at every attempt to claim their right they had been thwarted by the roar of the British lion. Only during the prelude to the Great War did the British at last offer to withdraw their resistance if Russia came in on their side against Germany. He waved his hand around him and told me to look well at how 'Tsargrad' had at last been conquered, full to bursting with Russian nobility, hocking their silver pommelled swords and chests full of medals for the price of a loaf of bread and how they filled the streets like so many scuttling rats. His eyes filled with tears as he finished by saying that the double headed eagle of the Romanovs and Byzantium had been consumed in a Bolshevik fire before it could rightfully fly again over its capital city."

When Ambassador Morgenthau bent forward to see the President's reaction to this anecdote he saw him deep in thought staring at the façade of the White House.

"Mr President, if you feel that this enough for today, let me continue with my report on another occasion."

President Wilson, directed his stare from the building to the Ambassador instead. He shook his head as if to wake himself and turned and waved at the service table.

"Have something to drink first and then continue. Excuse me if I appeared distracted but I have become entranced by the lust of these nations for the 'Queen of Cities'. Please continue Ambassador."

The Ambassador helped himself to some orange juice, and after taking a sip sat down to continue his account.

"On the deck of a battleship anchored off the small port of Mondros in the Sea of Marmara, the Turks signed the ceasefire and in effect their surrender on 29th October 1918. Ten days later the allies' battleships passed through the Dardanelles the very place that less than four years earlier they had failed to do at such cost, loosing twelve ships and hundreds of thousands of troops in the process. Now, unhindered they sailed to Istanbul and laid anchor in front of the Sultan's palace at Dolmabahçe. The time had come for the victors to squabble over the spoils.

It was the British who were to claim the lion's share, but with the Russians prematurely absent from the victors' team photograph, the balance of claims shifted. The French, the Italians and even the Greeks had plans to keep the city for themselves. I had a first hand account of this when I attended a reception at the British Embassy in Pera House. I saw the French and Italian heads of mission deep in an animated conversation and I decided to join them to see what they were discussing. When I approached they greeted me warmly and said my appearance had been timely and that they would like to sound me out on something. I, naturally, agreed. It was the Frenchman, Bompard, who spoke the stronger English and he began by saying that although the United States was the youngest of the great powers it was clear that with its resources and industry that the future lay in its hands. These same resources, industry and manpower were noticeable in the way they decided the fate of the Great War. The problem was that nothing in the 'Old World' could ever escape the bonds of history. The 'New World', he said, could never comprehend the roots of a conflict that went back over a thousand years.

We the victors were gathered there in that historic city but the discussion I had become part of was about who actually had the rightful historic claim to that city. Bompard said it was categorically not the English nor the Greeks, however entertaining the 'Hellenes' might look in their white skirts and shoes with red pompoms. He went on demonstratively that the 'Latins', France and Italy's, claim to the city was indisputable. It was the Latin Fourth Crusade of seven hundred years before that had removed the heretical Orthodox yoke from the city. The following fifty seven years had seen the Latin rite performed in the churches and freedom proclaimed in the lands of the Eastern Roman Empire as well as in its capital Constantinople. Tragically they had fallen back into the hands of the inept and ungrateful heretics who capitulated in the face of Turkish expansion a mere hundred and two years later. They went on to say that now the Turks had been vanquished it was their divine right to re-establish Latin sovereignty in the city. He finished by saying that the Greeks carried their thousand years of enmity towards the West like a banner accusing the Latins of treachery to our civilization and heresy to our religion but that I should pay them no attention. He added that if America were to support the Franco-Italian claim to Istanbul, American companies would be sure to benefit from the re-construction of the city. I thanked them for the goodwill and esteem they held our country in and I also said I was grateful for the history lesson and with a somewhat supercilious grin made my excuses and left.

It would be true to say that the British had backed the wrong horse once again in this Asia Minor adventure. They wanted to use the modern puppet Greek kingdom, that through centuries of feeling sorry for themselves had broken any link with the glory of ancient Greece, as a lever to serve their interests in Western Anatolia. They came rushing to the aid of that spoilt brat of the Paris Agreement, Venizelos, by arming his rabble of an army and landing them at Izmir on the 15th May 1919.

By that point the British were confident that they had successfully divided the Ottoman Empire amongst the victors. They succeeded in persuading the French and Italians to drop their claim to Istanbul, the French received as their spoils the region of Anatolia that was called Cilicia in ancient times; the Italians were awarded the Mediterranean region around Antalya. The British also had plans to set up Armenian and Kurdish states in Eastern Anatolia and similarly a Greek one at Pontus on the Black Sea. The purpose of this was to completely suffocate the Turkish enclave in Central Anatolia. Their tacticians realised only too late that this only went to stoke up the coals of Turkish nationalism and the sense of injustice that only further steeled the reserve of Mustafa Kemal and his companions.

In my honest opinion it was the poorly equipped Turkish Nationalists ability to hold the Greek army along the Sakarya river near Ankara in the summer of 1921 that sounded the death knell for the Allies' adventure in Asia Minor. After centuries of decline the Turkish people now found a new identity under the charismatic leadership of Mustafa Kemal. The decisive battle followed near Konya, where the nationalists, again poorly equipped and out numbered, annihilated the Greek army in only four days. There was a young American journalist called Ernest Hemmingway, who was covering the war from the Greek front who gave me a first hand account. He related how, before this decisive battle, the Greek officers attempted to raise their moral with outlandish claims and fantasies. I will repeat what he told me as it gives an insight into a mentality that hasn't budged since the siege of Constantinople some five hundred years before. On the night of the 25th August 1922, the Turks had taken up positions in the hills surrounding Afyon. Hemingway's account goes a long way towards explaining what the Greeks are now calling the 'Asia Minor Catastrophe'.

The officers to a man, including General Trikopis himself, were completely contemptuous of the Turks. They said that they were just ill-disciplined Central-Asian marauders who, given six months and even without firing not so much as a shot at them, could never get passed the Greek defence lines. These officers instead of preparing themselves for the expected Turkish attack of the following day looked to Dutch courage instead. Many a bottle of the Greek anisette, Ouzo, were consumed that night. Hemingway relates how a group of high ranking officers took him aside and told him that they wanted to confide to him something of great secrecy. They said that if he agreed to keep it quiet until the time came he would be the first journalist to break the story. Hemingway agreed and they revealed this to him.

King Alexander had died and the deposed king Constantine had been placed on the throne in his place. Prime minister Venizelos had also resigned. Both interpreted as omens that a new Byzantine dawn was breaking over the Great Hellenic homeland. The Turks were no longer the foe, they had now been confined to the waste heap of history. No, they said, the new foe were the allied powers who held the eternal city that had been Hellenic since the beginning of time.

They told Hemingway that the plan was not just auspicious it also had a perfect historical symmetry. King Constantine, who would take the title Emperor Constantine XIV, claimed his descent from the last Byzantine Emperor, whom some say to have been either the eleventh or thirteenth of that name, who so heroically and futilely defended Constantinople from Sultan Mehmed II. And so the 'new' Constantine would lead the Greek army on Constantinople, leaving just a few units to hold the Turks. Thus the victorious army of New Rome lead by the Emperor Constantine XIV would advance on the capital via Bursa. They would approach the city by the *Via Ignatia* and enter the walls via the triumphal arch of the Golden Gate (*Porta Aurea*) driving the English and Latins before them. The Emperor would perform his ablutions at the Studion Monastery, a symbolic cleansing of the spirit of Byzantium and its re-baptism before a triumphant march to Hagia Sophia where he would watch the crescent brought down from the mighty dome after five hundred years to be replaced by a golden cross. Hemingway said that they told him this in all seriousness and even offered him, as a fairly young journalist, first hand coverage of their fantastic venture!

A venture that disappeared as quickly as the morning mist when the Turkish guns started to open fire. The Greeks were routed as they abandoned their positions and scrambled back to Smyrna. Young Hemingway was obliged to join them in their flight. The Turkish infantry was pouring down from the Afyon hills like a landslide and advancing without hindrance. Hemingway managed to throw himself in the back of British truck and made good his escape.

Ambassador Morgenthau paused and took a deep breath and both men smiled at this peerless example of hubris. They sat for a while in silence before the President sat up in his chair and signalled for his secretary to approach from where he lingered under a cherry tree, he turned to Ambassador Morgenthau.

"Our throats are dry again, I will ask Jim to bring us something more conducive, some Port perhaps." He gave the instructions to his secretary who had practically bounded across the lawn and then turned back to the ambassador.

"There is one event that happened next that I have never been able to comprehend. After Mustafa Kemal's victorious army entered the city of Izmir, why on earth did they put the torch to it. After all it was a rich prize and they had taken it without hardly a shot being fired?"

Morgethau stroked his grey beard for a few seconds before offering an answer.

"The fire started in what was called the Frankish Quarter, the district where the rich Levantine community lived and, in particular, a large and wealthy Greek speaking community. Some said it was the fleeing Greek army that were the arsonists but I am inclined to agree with your view in that it was probably the victorious Turkish army that lit the first flame. And why? Well, Izmir, or Smyrna as it was then called, was the second city of the empire after Istanbul. It had such a large Levantine population the Turks named it 'Infidel Izmir' so even though it was Turkish in name it had, in practice, never been so; so this was an act of cauterisation, of wiping the slate clean so just as a new country would emerge phoenix-like out of the ashes of the Ottoman Empire, in the same way Izmir would rise again completely cleansed."

As President Wilson listened he nodded his head while at the same time gesturing to the butler to fill the glasses and give one to the Ambassador. Morgenthau who thanked the butler and then raised the glass to his lips before continuing.

"After that events unrolled at the speed of lightening. Having routed the invading Greek army and having seen them flee across the Aegean Sea they turned their attention to Istanbul and started advancing like a wave towards the city. After a tense few days the British announced that they would sign a ceasefire with the nationalist army and abandon the city. Even before Mustafa Kemal's army entered the city, they had sent their own officials to relieve the Ottoman ones of their duties and install their own police force to maintain order. The whole world watched these events with breaths held. The English stuck to their bargain and first sent their troops to Gallipoli and then from there back to their own country.

For the Greek population of Istanbul the night of the 5th October 1922 must have held the same sense of fearful desperation as it had done nearly five hundred years before on the 28th May 1453. One could say that after two thousand five hundred years of rule by the Hellenes, the Romans, the Byzantines, the Latins and finally the Ottomans, the Eastern Roman Empire was giving up its last breath. One could also say that another crusade had all but sacked the 'Queen of Cities' in their futile attempt to reinstate some long redundant former past glory but in the process delivered it up from under the conquering hooves of the Turkish white steed. This was to be the last time that the wings of the double headed eagle would ever beat over the eternal city!"

They both smiled thoughtfully and took another sip of their Port before the Ambassador concluded his account.

"One evening shortly before I left, I took a stroll along the quay at Galata with my secretary to observe the numerous steamboats packed with the Anatolian Greeks who were part of the exchange of populations that was taking place following the Treaty of Lausanne. It was still and quiet except for the sound of a plaintive Greek folk song coming from one of the ships. The sad song of a an Anatolian Greek torn from the land of his birth all for the sake of the grandiose dreams of a few hotheads on the other side of the Aegean sea. I asked my secretary George, who was of Greek origin himself, what the meaning of the words was. He repeated the words in Greek and then translated them for me into English:

Eshe iya Panaghia,
Ta milisame
Oniro itane.
To Lizmon isame.'

Farewell Panaghia[23]
We loved, we dallied,
It was just a dream,
All must be forgotten.

Ambassador Morgethau raised his glass to his lips while the President thoughtfully ran his finger around the rim of his. He looked up and across the swathe of the White House lawn before adding thoughtfully.

"If you ask me and considering the circumstances, the British did the honourable thing in leaving the city to the Turks as they did. 'Ave Atque Vale'."[24]

23. According to the Eastern Orthodox tradition one of the attributes of the Virgin Mary, protector of the city.

24. 'Hail and Farewell'.

Bibliography

Constantinople, G.Young, New York, 1992.

Eski İstanbul Abidat ve Mebanisi, C. E. Arseven, İstanbul, 1989.

Fatih Sultan Mehmed, André Clot, İstanbul, 1991.

Fatih ve Fetih,E.Aydın, Ankara, 1997.

Harem 1-2, Ç. Uluçay, Ankara, 1992.

İnsanlık Tarihinde Yıldızın Parladığı Anlar, S.Zweig, Ankara, 1967.

İstanbul-The Imperial City, J.Freely, Londra, 1996.

İstanbul'un Fethi, F. Dirimtekin, İstanbul, 1994.

İstanbul'un Fethi, Kritovulos, İstanbul, 1967.

İstanbul'un Fethinin Yakın Sebepleri, H. İnalcık, Ankara, 1953.

İstanbul ve Osmanlı Uygarlığı, B.Lewis, İstanbul, 1975.

Konstantiniye Muhasarası Ruznamesi, Nicolo Barbaro, İFD, İstanbul, 1953.

Kostantiniye ve Ayasofya Efsaneleri, S. Yerasimos, İstanbul, 1993.

Mehmet the Conqueror and His Time, F.Babinger, Princeton, 1978.

Muhteşem Süleyman, André Clot, İstanbul, 1994.

XVI.-XVIII. Yüzyıllarda Osmanlı İmparatorluğu, R.Mantran, İstanbul, 1995.

Osmanlı Devletinde Kardeş Katli, M.Akman, İstanbul, 1997.

Osmanlı Devleti Tarihi, J. V. Hammer, İstanbul, 1983.

Osmanlı İmparatorluğu'nun Yükseliş ve Çöküş Tarihi, DimitriKantemir, İstanbul,1998.

Padişah Anaları, A. K. Meram, İstanbul, 1996.

Padişahların Kadınları ve Kızları, Ç.Uluçay, Ankara, 1992.

Strolling Through Istanbul, J. Freely, İstanbul, 1989.

Şehir Düştü, G. Phrantzes, İstanbul, 1992.

Tarih-i Ebu'l Feth, Tursun Bey, İstanbul, 1977.

Tarih-i Selanikî, Selanikli Mustafa Efendi, İstanbul, 1864.

The Fall of Constantinople, S.Runciman, Cambridge, 1965.

The Ottomans, A. Wheatcroft.

The Wilder Shores of Love, L.Blanch, New York, 1996.

Trebizon de Avant L'oubli, J. M. Scaron, Paris, 1990.

Uluç Reis, C. Ş. Kabaağaçlı, İstanbul, 1980.